CHINA AT THE CROSSROADS

WHAT THE THIRD PLENUM MEANS FOR CHINA, NEW ZEALAND AND THE WORLD

EDITED BY PETER HARRIS

VICTORIA UNIVERSITY PRESS
for the New Zealand Contemporary China Research Centre

VICTORIA UNIVERSITY PRESS
Victoria University of Wellington
PO Box 600 Wellington
http://vup.victoria.ac.nz/

Copyright © Editor and contributors 2014
First published 2014

This book is copyright. Apart from
any fair dealing for the purpose of private study,
research, criticism or review, as permitted under the
Copyright Act, no part may be reproduced by any
process without the permission of
the publishers

National Library of New Zealand Cataloguing-in-Publication Data

China at the Crossroads : what the third plenum means for China,
New Zealand and the world / edited by Peter Harris.
Includes index.
ISBN 978-0-86473-978-0
1. China—Politics and government—21st century—Congresses.
2. China—Economic policy—2000- —Congresses. 3. China
—Foreign relations—New Zealand—Congresses. I. Harris, Peter,
1947-
320.951—dc 23

Printed by Printstop, Wellington

Contents

Preface   5

Introduction   7
Peter Harris

Guest Speakers
China – Trading Up or Creating Dependency?   17
Tim Groser

A Changing China – Implications for New Zealand   27
Phil Goff

Keynote Speech
China at the Crossroads: The Third Plenum and China's Reform Challenges   37
David Shambaugh

Part One: Governance and Society
The Moral Basis of Party Rule under Xi Jinping, and the Party's Search for a System of Ethics in the 21st Century   51
Kerry Brown

The Third Plenum and Rural Property Rights: Significant Decisions in the Right Direction   57
Jonathan Unger

The Chinese Trade Union Federation at the Crossroads – Relaxing Control over Labour or Risking Labour Instability   64
Anita Chan

Civil Society and Social Welfare after the Third Plenum   72
Stephen Noakes

Part Two: Economic and Financial Affairs
Demographic Dividend to Reform Dividend: *Hukuo* Reform and Its Impact on Economic Growth in China   79
Cai Fang

Public Financial Management in China: Fiscal Decentralisation and the Challenge of Containing Local Government Debt   87
Christine Wong

China's Resource Demand, the Environment and Enterprise System Reform — 96
Ligang Song

Part Three: International and Regional Implications, Including for New Zealand

Chinese Foreign Policy in the Light of the Third Plenum, with Special Reference to New Zealand — 107
Zhai Kun

The Impact of the Third Plenum and Other Recent Policy Initiatives on the Asia-Pacific Region — 113
Li-Gang Liu

The Impact of the Third Plenum and Other Recent Policy Initiatives on New Zealand — 120
Cameron Bagrie

Sino-American Rivalries after the Plenum: New Zealand and Regional Responses — 125
Marc Lanteigne

Questions and Answers — 131

Summing Up
John McKinnon — 138
Peter Harris — 142

Conclusion
The Third Plenum and New Zealand — 145
Jason Young

A Note on Further Reading — 152

Biographies in Brief — 154

About the New Zealand Contemporary China Research Centre — 159

Editor's Acknowledgements — 160

Appendix: 'China at the Crossroads' Conference Programme — 161

Index — 163

Preface

This book is based on the conference that the New Zealand Contemporary China Research Centre held on 2 July this year (2014). The title of the conference was 'China at the Crossroads: What the Third Plenum Means for China, New Zealand and the World'. The Third Plenum in question was the Third Plenum of the Eighteenth Central Committee of the Communist Party of China (CPC), which took place in Beijing in November 2013. The Plenum was heralded in China as marking a critically important stage in China's current reforms, though some commentators were sceptical about that.

The topic of the conference was decided on in principle by the Advisory Board of the China Research Centre at its meeting in November 2013. It was the sixth in the series of Wellington Conferences on Contemporary China that the China Research Centre has organised annually since 2009.

The conference took place in the Hunter Building of Victoria University of Wellington. A schedule for the day-long conference is provided at the back of this book. It was open to the public and designed for an audience consisting of both specialists and non-specialists. It was attended by some 190 people from government, academia, the media and elsewhere.

The conference brought together an outstanding group of China specialists and speakers. There were two guest speakers from Wellington, as well as fourteen other speakers from the US, China, Australia and New Zealand. Biographical details of all the speakers and panel chairs are provided at the back of this book.

The main part of the conference consisted of three panels: one on governance and society, one on economic and financial affairs, and one on the Plenum's international and regional implications, including for New Zealand. Some of the speakers at the conference gave papers, while others spoke from notes. This book consists largely of transcripts of the conference's main presentations, as approved by the speakers concerned. It is divided into three main parts corresponding to the three panels of the conference. It serves as a record of the conference and, we hope, a stimulus to future discussion.

Introduction

Peter Harris

'Hold on to your hat!' That was how one China specialist greeted the news that the Third Plenum of the Chinese Communist Party's Central Committee was meeting in Beijing in November last year (2013). He shared the excitement that many felt at the prospect of the Plenum bringing the winds of change to Chinese policy-making. Chinese President Xi Jinping – also General Secretary of the Communist Party – and Premier Li Keqiang were still relatively new to their jobs, having been selected in 2012. The Plenum seemed just the chance for them to push Chinese reforms on to a higher stage, resolving some of the intractable difficulties that had arisen in the country's extraordinary rush to wealth during previous decades.

As Phil Goff, one of the guest speakers at our conference, remarked, two decades ago a conference in New Zealand on a plenary meeting of the Chinese Communist Party's Central Committee would have been quite extraordinary. But nowadays, given China's economic size and influence and the ever-greater importance of the China market for New Zealand goods, every major policy meeting in Beijing matters. And over the years Third Plenums have come to matter more than most, coming as they do at a point in the Chinese leadership cycle when Chinese leaders are new enough to their mandate not to be weighed down with day-to-day cares.

The legendary Third Plenum of the 11th Central Committee of the Communist Party of China, held in December 1978, set the precedent. It was at that meeting that the twice-disgraced Party leader Deng Xiaoping took power again, and declared an end to Maoist political turmoil and the beginning of China's opening up and reform. What's often forgotten today is that in doing so Deng was not tackling reform with an entirely new blueprint for the future. He was drawing on a rough idea about China's development that had been agreed on by moderate Communist Party leaders in the 1950s and early 1960s. His vision of the future was also in many ways quite unspecific. Former German Chancellor Helmut Schmidt later recalled that when he met Deng and asked him about his blueprint for reform, Deng replied disarmingly that he had none, but was simply learning about things as he went along. It's from about that time that Deng's famous phrase about 'crossing the river by feeling for the stones underfoot' (*mozhe shitou guo he* 摸着石头过河) came into circulation. So the 1978 Third Plenum set the precedent for other Third Plenums, and for reform, but without having startling new solutions and without offering detailed prescriptions.

Later Third Plenums also marked significant stages in China's reform process. The Third Plenum in November 1993, for example, endorsed the phrase 'socialist market economy', thus reaffirming China's commitment to market-oriented reform after the chilly and uncertain period following the 1989 Tiananmen crisis.

So in November 2013 expectations were high. But when the Third Plenum finished its meeting and issued its Communiqué there was widespread disappointment. The Communiqué seemed to consist largely of vague generalities with few clear or precise policy initiatives. There was, admittedly, mention of the 'decisive role of the market in allocating resources', later described as a major point decided on by the Plenum. There was also an announcement that two new bodies were being created, both apparently significant and both (as we learned later) chaired by President Xi. These were the Council of State Security – often referred to as the National Security Council, since its Chinese name (*guojia anquan weiyuanhui* 国家安全委员会) is the same as the Chinese name given to the National Security Council in the US and elsewhere – and the Leading Group for Comprehensively Deepening Reform, thought to be the most ambitiously framed of any such inter-agency 'leading group' ever set up in Beijing.[1] But otherwise the Communiqué seemed to offer slim pickings.

Soon after that, though, things changed. The full texts of the Plenum's main documents were released, and commentators started to take a more positive view. The texts concerned were the Plenum's 'Decision . . . on Some Major Issues Concerning Comprehensively Deepening the Reform' and the 'Explanatory Notes' on the Decision provided by President Xi. The Decision, consisting of 60 Articles in 16 sections, was clearly an ambitious policy statement, as lengthy as any put out by the Party since its reform programme began. But how truly significant would it really turn out to be? Here views and interpretations differed, not helped by the often turgid prose in which the Decision was expressed.

The Decision is made up of four main elements. The first consists of specific policy changes, none of them systemic, but all providing for modest improvements in current conditions. Two of our conference speakers, our keynote speaker David Shambaugh and Li-Gang Liu from ANZ Bank, provided us with helpful comments on these. They include not only the creation of the two new bodies mentioned above, but also a decision to modify the one-child policy, the abolition of the controversial 'reform through education' labour camp system, and a provision for state-owned enterprises (SOEs) to contribute more substantively to the public welfare budget.

The second element of the Decision – and this is a very large part of it – consists of expressions of intent about policies that are already being put gradually into effect. Thus in the field of financial reform there is a pledge to further open financial

---

1   And one that since the Third Plenum has apparently had a busy life. One of our conference speakers, Christine Wong, noted that the Leading Group has six sub-groups covering the economy, ecology, the environment, etc, and is currently dealing with at least 336 policy initiatives distributed somewhat unevenly among the six groups.

markets, promote equity financing and develop the bond market, accelerate interest-rate liberalisation and accelerate renminbi capital account convertibility. These are all policies that in one form or another are already under way.

Similarly, in regard to social welfare there is a commitment to promote and regularise pension arrangements, and to push for the comprehensive reform of public health provision. Again, these build on existing policy reforms. In relation to managing the huge flow of people from the countryside into China's burgeoning cities there is reference to a new type of 'people-oriented urbanisation' and to accelerating reform of the *hukou* 户口 (household registration) system – both policies now being developed, though on a piecemeal basis, as discussed by our conference speaker Cai Fang. And with respect to the military, there are important provisions for improving the quality of the People's Liberation Army (PLA), including through the setting up of joint commands, so as to ensure that the PLA is 'loyal to the Communist Party of China' (an echo of Xi Jinping's reported concerns on that score in light of how the Red Army behaved when the Soviet Union collapsed in 1991). These provisions are likely to further strengthen the PLA Navy and Air Force, with strategic implications for the West Pacific rim and beyond.

The third element of the Decision consists of policies not yet put in place, but outlined or proposed for the first time. Among these are a number that are expressed in a provisional or somewhat vague manner. For example, there is a provision for judicial reform that is clearly designed to lessen official interference in the courts. But it refers only to 'explor[ing] ways to establish a judicial jurisdiction system that is appropriately separated from the administrative divisions'. Similarly, there are expressions of intent about preventing the torture and ill treatment of detainees, improving the Party's powerful Discipline Inspection Commission, curbing corruption – an overridingly important concern of the Xi Jinping administration – and stopping the relatives of officials benefiting from these officials' positions, though without any very detailed account of how these provisions will be put into effect.

There are also statements of intent with regard to improvements in natural resource pricing – a vital step not just financially but also ecologically, as our conference speaker Ligang Song made clear – as well as centre-local fiscal relations, budgeting and taxation, with a pledge to 'further rationalise the division of revenues' between central and local governments through tax reform. But this last pledge does not explain much more about this potentially critical field, in which, as our conference speaker Christine Wong explained, inadequate local governance revenue from the central authorities has created a debt problem that is hard to solve. One step the Decision does provide for, and which was highlighted by our conference speakers Li-Gang Liu and John McKinnon, is for local governments to finance themselves partly by issuing bonds, a measure that has since been put into effect in a pilot scheme in ten locations.

Mr Tony Browne, Executive Chair of the New Zealand Contemporary China Research Centre, opening the conference

The fourth element of the Decision – and this is a major part of it in a negative sense – is what it does not include. The emphasis of the Decision is on the economic and the incremental. Sweeping or systemic reforms are not in evidence, and the parts of the Decision that deal with social and in particular political affairs leave much unsaid. In the economic field there is little discussion of the role of state-owned enterprises (SOEs), whose privileged status, it is often argued, remains a major impediment to reform and to enhancing the role of the private sector. Instead the Decision declares roundly that 'public ownership playing a dominant role . . . is an important pillar of the socialist system with Chinese characteristics'. And while some consideration is paid to measures to prevent the unfair expropriation of land from farmers for urban development, a major cause of unrest and disquiet, strong measures seem to be missing.

On the social and political side, the Plenum Decision gives scant consideration to labour conditions, another cause of the local unrest that so often disturbs China nowadays, and a topic discussed in full by our conference speaker Anita Chan. As far as the Communist Party itself is concerned, old nostrums about the Party's mass line and about the role of the notional non-Communist parties represented in the ineffectual second house of the Chinese parliament, the CPPCC (Chinese People's Political Consultative Conference) are restated, and in some senses reinstated. These are the only concessions to the idea of participatory democracy, which is otherwise

Professor Neil Quigley, Deputy Vice Chancellor (Research) at Victoria University of Wellington, making opening remarks

ignored. Nothing is said about political pluralism or diversity – a point raised by our conference keynote speaker David Shambaugh. Instead there is an emphasis on loyalty to the Party and its role in 'realis[ing] the Chinese dream of a great revival of the Chinese nation' – 'China dream' being the watchword of the Xi administration. Structural impediments to justice such as the Party's notorious parallel – and secretive – system of investigating wrongdoers, known as *shuanggui* 双规, are also left unmentioned. And foreign policy, admittedly never acknowledged to be part of the Plenum's concerns, does not get a mention, even though the creation of the Council of State Security and reform of the PLA beg questions about changing foreign policy needs and priorities, some of which were addressed by two of our conference speakers, Zhai Kun and Marc Lanteigne.

There can be little doubt about the seriousness of intent of the Plenum's leading participants, including President Xi himself. The Plenum Decision makes no bones about the dilemmas and problems facing China at this stage of its growth. The Decision acknowledges that China's development 'has entered a new phase, and its reform has entered a period of overcoming major difficulties and a deepwater zone' (a reference, it seems, to Deng Xiaoping's old remark about crossing the river by feeling for the stones – the implication being that the river is now too deep for stones underfoot to be a guide). And in his Explanatory Notes Xi repeats the cautionary, even pessimistic phrase first used – as our speaker Christine Wong reminded us – by former Premier Wen Jiabao, namely that China's development is currently 'unbalanced, uncoordinated and unsustainable'.

But assessing the Plenum's overall significance and impact, partly in light of subsequent developments, has been hard to do. Both in China and elsewhere in the world opinion has ranged from the affirmative to the unconvinced. Some have seen the Plenum as opening the door to a raft of quite major reforms, not only through specific policy proposals but also by means of its overall mood and tone, and by the firm primacy it places on the role of the market. These optimists see the Chinese economy, and the Chinese market, growing steadily, albeit in a gradually evolving form that gives increasing primacy to Chinese consumers, new patterns of trade, and flows of outward investment. The trade – and investment – implications of this kind of development for New Zealand and other countries in the Asia-Pacific region are largely positive. There are admittedly aspects of such steady development that might be less positive – China's growing soft power, the state of US-China relations, and China's stance with regard to regional disputes in the Pacific – but in these respects the consequences are as yet hard to predict.

On the other hand others fear that the Third Plenum's decisions are too cautious, often too vague, and likely to be hampered if not hamstrung by officials and interest groups whose positions might be threatened. If these pessimists are right, China may face a prolonged period during which an imbalanced economy combined with continued political stresses and strains – among workers and farmers, among ethnic minorities in Tibet and Xinjiang, and among other groups frustrated by the country's pervasive corruption – are likely to make the country's politics, and so its overall economic and social condition, less easy to foresee. In this case the consequences for New Zealand and other countries in the region would inevitably be less predictable too.

It was partly with such divergences of views in mind that the New Zealand Contemporary China Research Centre took the advice of its Advisory Board and arranged a conference on 'China at the Crossroads – What the Third Plenum Means for China, New Zealand and the World'. It would be satisfying to say that a consensus about the Third Plenum emerged from the conference, which brought together leading academics and practitioners in the China world. But as the presentations published in this book show, there were in fact considerable differences of opinion. These range from those of David Shambaugh, who took a cautiously sceptical view and concluded by saying that he 'want[ed] to see the details' of the implementation of policy proposals, to those of Li-Gang Liu, who took an altogether more upbeat view.

It is reasonable to say, though, that most of the conference speakers thought that the Plenum, while offering some creative initiatives, did not go far enough, especially in such fields as centre-local fiscal relations, SOE reform, *hukou* reform, land rights and labour, not to mention politics and law. There was a general sense,

Introduction

too, that the Plenum and subsequent policy developments leave unanswered a number of important questions about the next phase of China's reforms, and of China's engagement with the world, including New Zealand. This is not perhaps as clear-cut and final a conclusion about the conference as many of us would have liked; but provisional assessments are perhaps only to be expected at this stage, given that – as our speaker Zhai Kun pointed out – President Xi Jinping is less than two years into a probable ten-year term.

Part of the audience in the Council Chamber of the Victoria University Hunter Building before the start of the conference

To consider the topic of New Zealand and the Third Plenum in more detail, my colleague Jason Young, Programme Director at our Centre, has contributed a concluding essay to this book which adds to what our conference speakers said on the subject. Before you read his essay, though, I hope you have time to go through the various speeches and presentations that form the bulk of the book. Whether or not you actually attended the conference you will, I think, find them interesting, sometimes provocative and always full of insights, just as we would expect from the calibre of the contributors. They form part of a conversation about China's reforms, and about China and New Zealand, which our Centre will, we hope, help sustain in an engaged and informed manner in the months and years to come.

GUEST SPEAKERS

The conference's two guest speakers, The Hon. Tim Groser, Minister of Trade, and The Hon. Phil Goff MP, a former Minister of Foreign Affairs and Trade, set the scene for the conference by emphasising the very positive nature of New Zealand's relationship with China, especially the two countries' rapidly expanding trade relations. The Hon. Tim Groser argues that New Zealand's flexible, market-oriented policies maximise opportunities and minimise any risk that might arise from China now being New Zealand's number one trading partner. The Hon. Phil Goff reviews the policy proposals of the Third Plenum and argues that while it is still too early to judge them, if they are put into effect New Zealand will be among those that benefit from them.

China – Trading Up or Creating Dependency?

The Hon. Tim Groser, Minister of Trade

Thank you for this opportunity to address the New Zealand Contemporary China Research Centre at my old alma mater, Victoria University.

I of course understand there are other pathways to relative professional success than tertiary qualifications. But having a great education from an excellent university is certainly one of them. I have never forgotten that. Nor have I forgotten one or two of the key professors of this university who helped me so much as a young man.

Back to China. So we have just passed – one year ahead of schedule – a milestone that frankly I thought was quite a stretch when Prime Minister Key and Premier Wen decided on it in Beijing in 2010: to double our two-way trade by 2015. Well, copy that: we put a positive tick beside that goal last week. Apparently, our leaders will not allow us to take a breather – the Prime Minister and the new President of China, President Xi, have now decided to lift the bar again. The goal now is to lift two-way trade to $30 billion by 2020.

By the way, our extraordinary success with China, which has both a political and a commercial side to it, is being noticed and admired – maybe even envied – around the world. In Mexico City, about ten days ago, and on my way to representing New Zealand at the heads of state meeting of a new trade grouping called the Pacific Alliance, I was holding a seminar on global trends in trade with my host, the Mexican Minister of the Economy and a former professor of economics, Dr Ildefonso Guajardo. This subject came up from the floor in the Q&A. When I gave the questioner the basic data on our exports, the Mexican Minister said New Zealand's exports were greater than Mexico's total exports to China. Mexico is the fourteenth largest economy in the world and has 118 million people.

Take a bow, New Zealand Inc. It has taken a lot of people and a lot of hard work over a number of years over successive governments to get us to this excellent position. We are now seeing the benefits in terms of increased export income (and thus lower foreign borrowing than would otherwise have been the case), more jobs, and higher economic growth. If we stick to what we know works in terms of foreign policy, trade policy and the domestic economic policies that underwrite this huge success, the future is even brighter.

This very success is, however, giving rise to a number of people asking a question – namely, are we in danger of creating too much trade dependency on China?

Personally, I think it would be harsh to brush this aside by saying some people can only ever look at a glass as half-empty. It is a fair question that deserves a fair answer. It is especially so in the light of the defining event of our trading economy in the last fifty years: the body-blow we suffered when the UK, which then absorbed 50 per cent of our total exports, entered the then EEC (European Economic Community), triggering a whole series of difficult adjustments by New Zealand. As a country, we know the hard way about trade dependency and the risks it involves.

However, as I go through my analysis of the issue, just bear in mind one central fact. The world is utterly different today than it was in the 1970s. The front and centre of the problem faced forty years ago by New Zealand trade negotiators like me, and particularly the people I learned my craft from, was we had too much product for export and too few market opportunities open to us. The world just shut us out.

Today's trade policy 'problem' – if indeed 'problem' is the right word for it – is the opposite: we have more opportunities than we could ever exploit. In terms of our agri-business exports, we can only feed around 40–50 million people. The new trade agenda in front of us – and TPP (Trans Pacific Partnership) is the biggest game in town here – is about risk diversification and giving our companies more choice still.

It is not just, to use American basketball parlance, 'defence' (i.e. risk diversification) but 'offence' as well – we want to strengthen the hand of our export sales managers when they look at alternative markets for the world-class suite of goods and services their company and New Zealand have to offer. If you don't have choice, you don't have a negotiating position – you have a set of requests. I remember one veteran Australian trade negotiator telling me as a young New Zealand negotiator in Canberra that 'New Zealand negotiates through a veil of tears'. It was meant to intimidate me, so I just said, 'You're right. But aren't we good at it.'

Well, we are also good – very good – at the new game where, thanks to our successes married to economic development in the emerging economies, we are in an entirely different and utterly more favourable position. In addition to the two 'jewels in the New Zealand trade policy crown' of CER (Closer Economic Relations) and the China FTA (Free Trade Agreement), we have an FTA with

Hong Kong, a comparable agreement with Taiwan (another world first), a comprehensive FTA with the whole of ASEAN (AANZFTA)[1] that was finally ratified by Indonesia, the largest ASEAN economy, in 2011, an FTA with Chile, P4 (or Pacific Four – the foundation stone of TPP) and several individual FTAs with individual Southeast Asian countries. And we are still benefiting enormously from the Uruguay Round set of agreements that twenty years ago brought some discipline to export subsidies and stabilised a number of market-access issues important to New Zealand.

I am not describing our negotiating agenda here – TPP, the Pacific Alliance, other current negotiations. The trade agreements I have just referenced are all done and impacting positively on our country. But we are the Oliver Twist of trade policy. We are hungry for more. When we say 'We are ambitious for New Zealand' it is more than a good political bumper sticker. We mean it.

Defining the 'Dependency' Issue
There are two associated 'dependency' issues which should be considered before we get to the main course, but I don't think we need to spend a lot of time on them. The first is what is called 'indirect dependency' on China. That is, that adverse developments in China would impact on Australia and our other major trading partners and thus indirectly on New Zealand. The second, though hardly front of mind, relates to 'dependency' on imports, given that China is our largest source of imports and these will be an important part of the supply chain for thousands of our businesses.

The issue of indirect dependency is an issue, particularly when you take into account what I call 'the triangulation' of the NZ-Australia-China economic relationship. It arises because of the intersection of two facts:

- Australia is actually a larger market for New Zealand exports today than China when you take into account our exports of services to Australia and add that to our exports of merchandise. So anything that affects the Australian economy adversely will, by definition, affect New Zealand. Putting all hackneyed trans-Tasman jokes aside, purely for economic reasons a strong Australia is fundamentally in New Zealand's interests.

- Australia is far more exposed than New Zealand to a downturn in China, given the vast size of its mineral exports to China. The long-signalled shift in emphasis by the Chinese authorities from investment-led to consumption-led growth (this long predates the fascinating reform directions of the Third Plenum) is already affecting 'hard' commodities, and these are Australia's export strength.

---

1   AANZFTA is the ASEAN (Association of Southeast Asian Nations)-Australia-New Zealand Free Trade Association – ed.

The Hon. Tim Groser, Minister of Trade, making a guest speech

So, there definitely is a danger of 'indirect dependency' here, especially through the triangulation of the NZ-Australia-China economic relationship. But consider the following.

There are rather large practical limits to what we can do about this. Even further diversification of our export effort (which is central to this Government's trade policy) does not avoid the problem. An astonishing 124 countries now count China as their number-one trading partner. If China slows down or worse, all our export markets slow down. Period. We would be adversely affected even if we did not sell a single dollar of goods and services directly to China.

At market exchange rates, China is expected to pass the US in terms of economic weight around 2020. We used to say 'When the United States catches a cold, the world starts to sneeze'. Correct. Just add the words 'or China' to that phrase and we are where New Zealand always was: a small economy whose economic fortunes will always be affected by global downturns in the major economies of the world. On this question of 'indirect dependency', I am tempted to say 'yes, but tell me something I don't know'.

What is important for New Zealand is to maintain a flexible set of economic, market-oriented policy instruments to adjust to external shocks, wherever those external shocks come from. And those signals need to impact immediately on economic actors' decisions – not five years too late when officials and politicians have finally woken up to the fact that the comfortable world around them has changed and this demands policy readjustment. That includes sticking with a flexible exchange rate, avoiding returning to misplaced subsidies in the hope that they provide 'certainty', having competitive energy pricing, good infrastructure and so on. Having a 'competitive economy' is a good shorthand way of putting it.

One of the reasons, though by no means the sole reason, why the disappearance of the UK – a far more dominant market for New Zealand then than China today – hit us so hard was because we had economic policies in place that came straight out of the manual for a 'command economy'. Those hopeless domestic policies vastly complicated the adjustment we had to undertake. Of course, I recognise that there is a whole bunch of people out there who don't get this and are offering New Zealanders a fast policy ride back to the future. Well, to those folk, I would encourage them to reflect a little more deeply, if they are politically capable of it.

We can deal quickly with the second issue – are we becoming too dependent on imports on China? First, recall that ultimately there is only one point in exporting to any country – to provide the foreign exchange to import or, if you have more than you need to pay for your current imports, invest the foreign exchange earned.

And here, as our number one source of imports, China continues to perform a huge positive role in providing New Zealand households and businesses with an increasingly sophisticated range of highly competitive goods and services that they buy from China. Presumably, New Zealanders and companies buy from China only because they believe China offers the best value for their money.

But if, at the margin, China became uncompetitive for whatever set of reasons, there is no real risk here to New Zealand. There is a global market out there we can turn to. It would just cost us a little more at the margin. No, this issue is not about any 'dependency' on China as a source of imports.

The Growth of New Zealand Exports
Three things have powered the extraordinary growth of New Zealand exports to China: the economic development of China, liberalisation of China's economy through its joining the WTO (World Trade Organization) and the bilateral New Zealand-China FTA, and the enormous efforts New Zealand Inc. has put in to leverage off the opening of the China market in recent years.

Sustained economic growth in China and the rise of disposable income is the most important by far. I won't quote any numbers. You all know them and have your own favourite 'China statistic' to quote. The only observation I would make is this: it took decades of growth of income in China before it made an economically significant difference to this small trading partner of China's that is New Zealand.

It is worth keeping this in the back of our minds, since I am optimistic we are going to see a whole variety of 'mini-China' stories play out on New Zealand as the extraordinary growth story in the emerging economies plays out, starting with economies like Indonesia, Brazil, Mexico, Turkey, the Gulf States, the Philippines and others. The biggest question of all is obviously India.

But development takes time before it has a large measurable impact on New Zealand. For the moment, our export story is very much a 'China story'. But we live in the era of 'hyper-globalisation' where the Petersen Institute has estimated that over the period 1990–2010, over seventy countries grew their per capita incomes at an annual rate well exceeding the rate of growth of US per capita income.

The second factor is of course the opening of the Chinese market through trade negotiations. Having hundreds of millions of consumers with disposable incomes ready to buy the sophisticated suite of goods and services that New Zealand can produce is not much use if you don't have access to them because of their trade barriers. Those very vocal New Zealanders whose views we read every day on this matter and who oppose every trade agreement I and other New Zealanders have tried to put together, including TPP, don't get this and they never will. I don't know how they think New Zealand is supposed to earn a living in the world.

The first decisive move in terms of our getting far better access to the increasingly well-off Chinese consumer was the conclusion of twelve years of negotiation in Geneva that allowed China to become a member (technically, to 'resume' membership) of the WTO. New Zealand was the first country to conclude bilateral WTO negotiations with China. At one level, therefore, this had nothing to do with our FTA: it is one of our 'four firsts',[2] as the Chinese leaders put it. But at a political level, it had a lot to do with our FTA. The Chinese did not forget this, and this was one of the political building blocks behind the FTA.

Finally, there is no difference between 'foreign policy' and 'trade policy' for New Zealand. Get it right, and they complement each other. Get one of them wrong, and it is like waving the wrong flag at a bull, so to speak.

The second decisive move was the signing of the FTA in 2008. This was a huge achievement and we today have a literally unique set of agreements in place: a comprehensive FTA with China, a comparable agreement with Hong Kong in place since 2010 and since 1 December last year, a comprehensive economic cooperation agreement with Taiwan.

Our exports to Taiwan have exploded since December, which is hardly surprising since duties were eliminated on entry into force on a very significant set of tariff lines. So if you think of the greater China economic zone, New Zealand is currently better placed than any other country in the world to get access to its consumers.

However, I have always said that an FTA, or an agreement like it by any other name, does not in itself put a dollar on the table, if you don't make efforts to use

---

2 The four firsts are: New Zealand's decision as a developed country to enter into FTA negotiations; the signing of the FTA; the New Zealand-China agreement on China's accession to the WTO (World Trade Organization); and New Zealand's recognition of China's status as a market economy – ed.

and leverage it. From the Prime Minister down, Ministers have put enormous effort into leveraging that effort in recent years – have a look at the visas in my passport as one sign.

And it is obviously not just Ministers: our companies and our institutions have lifted their game – sometimes a little late, in my view. We have established the New Zealand China Council, chaired by the Rt. Hon. Sir Don McKinnon. NZTE (New Zealand Trade and Enterprise), which has been given considerable new financing, is adding six staff to the sixty-two staff already on the ground in China. MPI (Ministry of Primary Industries) is in the process of moving from one to seven staff in China. Divisions working on China in New Zealand are being strengthened. It is a work in progress. Our footprint in China will presumably look quite a bit different ten years from now.

It is however beginning to pay off. From 1992 to 2007, merchandise exports to China increased by an average compound annual growth rate of 12 per cent. From 2008 to 2012 that rate more than doubled, to 28 per cent per annum. Last year, exports increased by a mind-boggling 45 per cent. Note, incidentally, that this was during a period when Chinese growth was 'slowing down'.

That growth rate has to slow. If you extrapolate our current rates of export growth, within a few years we would be exporting more than 100 per cent of our exports to China – a literal impossibility. With respect to our main agri-business exports, we will sooner or later hit supply constraints.

I have been a sceptic for some time of the conventional wisdom around the 'what happens if China's growth rate slows' school of thought. First, because it is not a question of 'if' – China will slow down. No country, with the singular exception of the city state of Singapore, has done otherwise from the industrial revolution onwards. Second, because it seems to me to miss the point.

What matters to China's trading partners is the increment of GDP growth, not some abstraction called a 'growth rate'. Today's China's GDP is around US$10 trillion and the rate of growth is around 7 per cent. Yesterday (metaphorically speaking – say 2005) it was half that – US$5 trillion growing at around 10 per cent. So today, the annual increment of growth is around $700 billion, far larger than the $500 billion GDP increment seven or eight years ago when China had double-digit growth.

Sectors 'Most At Risk'

I recently asked MFAT's Economic Division to undertake a more granular analysis of sectors of our export economy that were most 'trade exposed' to China. It is a pretty comprehensive study, so I will draw out only a few of what I think are the key conclusions we should draw from it. Nor will I try to explain their choices of metrics and methodologies. They all look sensible to me. Before joining the dark side and going into politics some ten years ago, I used to do this sort of analysis myself.

There are eighteen products that are highly 'trade-exposed' to China (meaning overweight in trade terms). In 2012, their combined export value was $5.25 billion, comprising 77 per cent of our exports to China that year. In seventeen of the eighteen 'most at risk' products, exports grew faster to China in 2012 than the same set of products to the rest of the world. And in some cases we are seeing rapid growth in exports to China associated with declines in New Zealand exports to the rest of the world.

There is clear evidence of market-switching going on. Crustaceans are among the 'highly trade-exposed' categories. Should we be concerned that our exports of crustaceans to the world excluding China fell in 2012? It is not obvious to me why we should be concerned: our exports to China increased by 28 per cent. China is simply paying higher prices.

But, you ask, what if China Inc. decides eating crustaceans is 'soooo 2012', and the in-crowd in Shanghai starts eating escargots? What then happens to our crustacean exporters?

Well, I would have thought it was pretty obvious – our crustacean exports (heavily represented, by the way, by Maori business interests who are going really well in the Chinese market) go back to the other markets and take a price hit. They would not like it, but it is hardly the end of the world. And since we have a market economy, someone, somewhere in Aotearoa, will think – 'I wonder if we could export escargots to Shanghai?'

Sheepmeat is another example and of far greater economic importance to our export earnings. When we concluded the Uruguay Round negotiations (and the numbers are ingrained on my mind twenty years on), we bound the figure of 225,000 tonnes of access into WTO law at zero duty. Our exports of sheep meat to China exploded in 2013 – they grew 95 per cent to a tad under $600 million. As a consequence, we are selling way short of that legally permissible 225,000 tonne figure to the EU. So what do you think would happen to our sheep meat exports if China Inc., for some incalculable reason, said 'we have gone off New Zealand sheep meat'? Well, we are in a university. I will let you work out yourself the answer to today's assignment.

We can see the same thing starting to happen to beef. The figures for CY (calendar year) 2013 show declining exports of New Zealand to many markets. But they also show an astonishing 374 per cent increase in beef exports to China to over 35,000 tonnes. No wonder Sir Graeme Harrison, the Chairman and founder of one of our largest export companies, says 'sheep meat is interesting, but for our meat industry, the real China play will be in beef'.

There are exports in this analysis where moving back to the next best-priced market would be very challenging. Iron ore is one of them. China consumes around two-thirds of the world's tradable iron and, unsurprisingly, 78 per cent of our iron ore exports go to China. But this is only 1 per cent of our exports to China. This is a huge issue for Australia. It is a much lesser issue for NZ. But recall the earlier point about the triangulation of the NZ-Australia-China trade flows.

Conclusions
So what general conclusions can we draw here, and what policies should we have in place to take some of the risk out of this situation?

The first and most obvious point is that the core external challenge facing New Zealand is to lift our export performance in a sustained way – hence the emphasis the Government places on export markets in our Business Growth Agenda, and its desire to lift the ratio of exports to GDP by ten percentile points by 2025. This is the only way to reduce our addiction to OPM (borrowing Other People's Money) and paying our way in the world. As the Prime Minister has said 'We have proven we can spend like a first world country; now we have to prove we can earn like a first world country'. China is the most important part of a solution to that over-arching strategic challenge; it is not part of the problem.

Because of that we should try to export more, not less to China, and the Chinese are ready to welcome this – hence the agreement at the highest political level between Prime Minister Key and President Xi to the new goal of $30 billion two-way trade by 2025.

That said, it does always make sense to look at downside scenarios, while not being overwhelmed by them. If China, for whatever reason, had a deep and sustained economic crisis – and we know from the global financial crisis, the deepest downturn for seventy years for developed countries, that even the richest countries can take nothing for granted – we should accept the obvious: a large economic shock in China will negatively impact New Zealand.

If 124 countries have China as their largest trading partner, it is obvious that we would be negatively impacted even if New Zealand exported nothing to China. I recall saying in 1997, at the time of the then Asian economic crisis, that if your country was not affected by the Asian financial crisis it was a black mark against your country. It meant you had wasted the previous ten years and had failed to become integrated with the page 17 Asian success story. As far as I recall, only one economy remained gloriously unaffected by the Asian economic crisis of the late 1990s: North Korea. So what did that mean? We should have learned from North Korea?

The biggest single risk-minimisation strategy New Zealand can follow is to ensure that our exporters – whether they are exporting high technology medical equipment or infant formula – have access to other markets. That, ladies and gentlemen, is what our pro-active trade negotiation and trade promotion agenda is all about.

As always, New Zealand's trade negotiation agenda is agonisingly difficult to bring to a closure; I have never been associated with an 'easy' negotiation. Everything takes longer than planned. Every agreed time-line gets broken. Frustration is the rule, not the exception. It is unlikely you would get the chance, but if you did, ask the gentleman who was responsible for getting China back into the WTO. That took twelve years. His Russian counterpart (whom I know extremely well) took eighteen years – and there was talk in the Dumas of charging him and his colleagues with treason. The worst I suffer from is continual jet lag.

Absolutely the best insurance policy New Zealand can take out is to complete the TPP negotiations and improve our access to the huge markets that would represent – about 40 per cent of global GDP. And this allows me to return to where we started: the real, as opposed to the imagined, lessons of 1973 when our overwhelmingly important export market, the UK, started to turn away from New Zealand and legally required us to export less, year by year ('Protocol 18' was the name of this policy instrument). The real problem was not so much the dependency of our export base on the UK (which was around three times as high as the relative share of our exports to China today). The fundamental problem was twofold:

- We had no alternative markets – nobody had done very much about exploring what might lie east and south of the English Channel and what political and other relationships we might need to develop as a consequence;
- We had rigid economic policies in place designed to try and 'protect' everything but which ended up protecting nobody.

Ladies and gentlemen, we are in a far, far better space today. We should be celebrating, not fretting about, our economic linkages with China.

A Changing China – Implications for New Zealand

The Hon. Phil Goff, MP

Thank you very much. Ni hao, good afternoon and kia-ora tatou.

Mine has been a long relationship with China, going back some twenty-five years. I chose my first occasion to visit China auspiciously at the beginning of June 1989, when I found myself in the middle of Tiananmen Square, and have very vivid memories of the sad occasion that followed several days later. I've been back many times and developed good working relationships with Ministers such as Tang Jiaxuan and Li Zhaoxing, both former Foreign Ministers, a gentleman called Mr Bo Xilai, who has gone on to be even more famous than at the time I knew him and worked with him in negotiating the New Zealand-China Free Trade Agreement, and Minister Chen Deming. I have to say that over that period of time I have been incredibly impressed by the progress that has been made in China, and by the singular ability of that country to lift hundreds of millions of people out of poverty. Equally, there are values that China has that are different from ours, and the nature of our relationship has been that we've been able to discuss those quite frankly without unfortunately being able to resolve the differences.

I was thinking as I was looking at the topic of this conference that two decades ago to have a conference addressing the Central Committee of the Chinese Communist Party's plenary decisions in a particular year would have been quite extraordinary. The fact that we are here today doing that indicates the rapidity in the growth of China's economic strength and its importance to us as a trading partner, and indeed its importance to the world.

Two years ago China became our largest trading partner and the largest export market for our goods. Just last week, two-way trade between our countries exceeded $20 billion. By 2020, it could easily exceed $30 billion on present growth projections.

Growth in demand for high quality, safe and protein-rich food by China's growing middle class has been absolutely phenomenal. Last year, the sale of NZ dairy goods in China grew from $2 billion to $4 billion in one year – it doubled.

Trade in New Zealand logs peaked at $1.7 billion, but as an indication of how you can't be complacent and relaxed about how the market will develop, that has now sharply declined as growth in investment in infrastructure in China has been wound back.

Sheep meat exports – and as a farmer with a huge flock of sixty sheep(!) I pay particular attention to these things – have moved from 1 per cent of all of our lamb exports in 2009 to 35 per cent last year, valued at $670 million. Beef exports last year alone jumped 271 per cent to $190 million, with a huge expansion likely, I believe, in that area. The figure that really astonished me as a crayfish lover is that we exported $240 million's worth of live crayfish to China last year. Almost every crayfish that went out of New Zealand ended up in a restaurant in China, and I think some of the iwi authorities are doing very well out of that.

Growth in services has similarly been spectacular. For quite a long time now China has been our biggest single market for international students, some 24,000 a year. That came as the result of an initiative I took, an amendment to the Education Act in 1989 which allowed universities and educational institutions to take in foreign fee-paying students. I took a lot of flack for that at the time, but it is a $2.6 billion dollar industry and I'm proud of that amendment. Tourism has again grown spectacularly. There was a time when the numbers were tiny, when people would come on three-day tours, go to carefully selected shops, do their shopping, then be rushed off to Australia or somewhere else. Today tourism is around a quarter of a million a year, growing rapidly, making China our second biggest source of tourists, with high-quality Chinese tourists spending around $3,400 each on their visit here.

All of that paints a very obvious picture. The growth that has occurred in China as a market has been incredibly valuable to us. At a point when the world was submerged in the global financial crisis and our markets in the United States and Europe were shrinking, it was the growth in the China market that kept New Zealand from dropping down into the crisis levels of economic recession that other countries in the west faced.

There is another side to this story. That is that New Zealand has developed an increasing level of dependence on a narrow range of products and one market. That understandably causes concern. Never put all of your eggs into one basket.

China today takes 23 per cent of our total exports, up astoundingly from about six per cent in 2010. That is still a long way from the level of dependence that we had on the United Kingdom back in the 1950s and '60s. But my guess is that within ten years we will be at the level of dependence on China as a market that we were on the United Kingdom at the time it went into the European Community in 1974 – that's about 30 per cent of our exports going into one market.

Indirectly we are even more dependent on China. The other reason we got through the global financial crisis was that the Australian market was booming on the basis of its exports of other commodities to China. China today is, I think, the largest trading partner of most of the countries in the Asia-Pacific region, and of 124 countries in total. It goes without saying that if for some inexplicable reason the Chinese economy was to collapse, the direct and indirect effects on New Zealand's trade and economy would be dire indeed.

The catalyst for the growth in trade was a high quality and comprehensive Free Trade Agreement that I signed in 2008 in the Great Hall of the People with the then Minister of Commerce Chen Deming. The timing was perfect. It coincided with the cumulative impact of decades of consistently high growth in the Chinese economy. That has produced an urban middle class of over 300 million people – figures vary from 200 to 600 million, but a mid-point would be about 300 million people – who have middle incomes. That makes it an even larger market for middle-income purchasers than the United States. They do have disposable incomes and are keen on safe, high-quality and protein-rich food.

That demand is, I think, likely to be sustained into the future. It's interesting that while demand for hard commodities like iron ore and coal is diminishing as the boom that was deliberately created by the Chinese Government to ward off the effects of the global financial crisis is now being wound down, the demand for soft commodities like dairy is continuing to increase.

China is unable to meet that demand internally. Six or seven weeks ago I was up at Yutian 3, the latest Fonterra dairy farm in Hebei province, and it was very interesting to see cows being milked four times a day, producing 34 litres of milk compared to our cows' average of 21–22 litres a day. I was wondering whether China was going to learn everything we could teach it and then out-compete us in our own field. I am advised by Fonterra and others that that is unlikely to happen – that agricultural land in China is not sufficiently available for that, that water is a scarce commodity and the current state of agriculture won't allow that to happen. As the Chinese increase their production of liquid milk the demand will rise even faster. One of the things I remember is a meeting I had with the then Premier Wen Jiabao. We were right in the midst of negotiations on the FTA and I was having trouble with the Ministry of Agriculture in China, and Wen Jiabao said to me here in Wellington, 'I want every child in China to drink a full glass of milk each morning'. And I looked at the Premier with a somewhat distraught look and said, 'Premier, I don't think we can manage that!'

But the demand is growing and I think we can be confident about that. I don't believe we can be equally confident that prices will stay where they are, and indeed I saw from the latest online market that dairy prices are falling. You can bet that when prices have been as high as they are, there will be new competitors from all over the world trying to get into that particular market.

The other warning for New Zealand is that we can't be complacent about being 100 per cent pure New Zealand. First of all the melamine crisis, which was largely focused within China – and actually perversely in a way, because Fonterra owned half of Sanlu and yet the crisis worked in our favour as Chinese parents demanded foreign-produced infant formula – but particularly the DCD[1] and the botulism scares have indicated that if we're complacent about how we market our goods then

---

1 Dicyandiamide, traces of which were found in Fonterra milk in late 2012.

we will suffer accordingly. Friends in Beijing read out to me what was being written at the time on Weibo.² Frankly the comments were disastrous for New Zealand's branding, with people talking about New Zealand's 'poisonous' foods. So my advice to the government would be, when you restructure and cost-cut and understaff MFAT (the Ministry of Foreign Affairs and Trade) and MPI (the Ministry of Primary Industries) don't expect that those sort of things are going to be risk-free. As we saw in China they proved not to be – real damage was done. And Fonterra must share responsibility for that in terms of poor communication and lack of strategy.

Aside from these issues, what are the risks of an economic crisis or downturn in the Chinese economy that might damage New Zealand, given our growing dependence on it? And will the reforms foreshadowed at the Third Plenum mitigate those risks?

Pessimists point to the slowing rate of growth in the Chinese economy. They point out that China is no longer increasing its share of the US and European import markets. They highlight growing debt levels, an appreciating currency where the RMB (renminbi) is 35 per cent up against the US dollar compared to 2005, and that China's low-cost advantage has been blunted by wages that have trebled in the past decade. They point to internal inefficiencies, bureaucracy and corruption undermining China's performance.

Much of that may be true, but those things should be seen in context. After thirty years of double-digit growth, it would be remarkable indeed if China's growth continued at that level. I was reading a *China Watch* article by David Mahon from Beijing the other day, and he pointed out that when growth in China was 9.2 per cent in 2009 it produced increased value of 2.7 trillion RMB. In 2013 growth had fallen 7.7 per cent but because it came from a much higher base, the added value was in fact 5 trillion RMB. I think that puts slower growth in context.

China's debt has gone up but as a percentage of GDP it is still lower than Germany's, the least indebted country in the G7.³

The New Zealand Treasury last year concluded that there are cyclical risks to China's economic performance in the medium term but that the risks were manageable.

The Reserve Bank of New Zealand in May of this year warned of the build-up of fragilities in the financial system in China. The so-called shadow banking sector runs higher risks than the more regulated and supervised banking sector. Local government financing vehicles face significant funding and liquidity risks. There is a risk of a sharp decline in property prices which could reduce household wealth and trigger more widespread asset losses in the financial sector.

The Reserve Bank warned that a contraction in Chinese demand could very obviously have a major impact on New Zealand's exports. However with a view

---

2   The Chinese microblogging site.
3   Group of Seven: Canada, France, Germany, Italy, Japan, the UK and the US.

to what happened at the Third Plenum it also noted that reforms that were being foreshadowed would liberalise interest rates, reform local government finances, improve transparency and regulate the shadow banking sector, and that would help address these risks. I think that is a justified analysis.

The central government in China holds extensive assets and foreign reserves. External debts are minimal and central government debt low. The Chinese government, it concluded, therefore has the capacity to intervene to stabilise financial markets and manage any risks.

The Third Plenum and the leadership of Xi Jinping mark a clear commitment by the new administration in China to address the need for economic, social and environmental reform.

The Hon. Phil Goff, MP, making a guest speech

Comparing it with the landmark reforms of Deng Xiaoping at the Third Plenum of 1978 may be an exaggeration. The 1978 reforms marked a complete change: the abandonment of Mao's disastrous economic policies and political management and a new platform to launch China's opening up and reform. The 2013 reforms, unlike those of thirty-five years earlier, build on preceding changes and mark an intensification of efforts to address outstanding problems.

The most significant change will be to allow the market to play a more decisive role in the allocation of resources, and to price those resources accordingly. There'll be curbing of the powers of SOEs (state owned enterprises) and new areas opened up for private sector investment and competition. Unnecessary red tape and regulation will be cut. Financial markets will be liberalised and improved and the tax system further reformed. (That reminds me of what we were doing in 1987 on a much smaller scale in New Zealand.)

I think the social reforms are also very significant. Most families will be able to have a second child if they choose – though people in Beijing were saying to me a few months ago, 'That's all very well, but you should see the prices of apartments in Beijing', so maybe it won't have as dramatic effect as we imagined. The *hukou* or household registration system will be reformed, not before time, to give rural migrants to the cities equal access to public services. Things from the 1950s like re-education through labour will be abolished.

The crackdown on corruption is, I think, one of the most interesting facets. Many of us thought, yes, that's what a new administration does – it says it's going to crack down, there's a big flurry, a display, then things quietly die down as vested interests reassert themselves. I was interested to see the figures from last year showing that 31,000 officials were arrested for corruption and a third of them sentenced to more than five years in prison, and that included people up to the highest levels including Politburo Members. The crackdown is being sustained and appears likely to continue to apply pressure to change an entrenched part of the culture.

There is a renewed commitment to addressing air, water and soil pollution caused by decades of subordinating the environment to rapid economic growth. And having breathed the air in Beijing that will also be not before time.

The reforms, however, don't embrace political liberalisation. Media censorship has been tightened and the pervasive and dominant role of the Party has been entrenched.

It remains to be seen whether the intent of reforms can be realised without the accountability that the rule of law, an independent judiciary, a free media and the upholding of human rights provide in a democratic society.

To conclude, I think it is too early to judge conclusively what impact the Third Plenum reforms will have on China's economy and society and therefore indirectly on us and the region. The need for reform is undoubted, the commitment to reform and the leadership of that reform is apparently strong, and the general direction of the reform seems to me to be very positive. The ability to implement it and whether the necessary reform goes far enough are both less certain.

New Zealand will benefit economically from the successful implementation of reform because of the high level of interaction between our economy and China's. So too will the regional and global economy.

I believe that New Zealand should seize the opportunities China offers us as a trading partner, and that we will also need to make changes to ensure we are best able to realise the full potential it offers. At the same time I think we would be wise to make strenuous efforts to diversify our export markets and the very narrow export base our country relies on. That is a commonsense safeguard against the risks that dependency on any one market or narrow range of products involves.

With reform and continuing economic success, China's influence over us, the region and the world will grow commensurately. Political and military power grows with economic power.

Our engagement with China, and the balancing of our relationships with China and the other superpower in our region, the United States, will more and more become front and centre of New Zealand's foreign and trade policy.

KEYNOTE SPEECH

Any overarching appraisal of the significance of the 2013 Third Plenum must provide an overview of the most significant challenges currently facing the Chinese people and Chinese policy-makers, so that the policy prescriptions of the Third Plenum can be reasonably assessed in light of them. Professor David Shambaugh provides this overview by discussing ten critical issues now facing China after the highly impressive achievements of its development during the last few decades. These issues are: chronic economic imbalances, including a strong rural-urban divide, social strains and inequities, widespread corruption, the need for political and legal reform, the stresses of rapid urbanisation, environmental pollution, the growth of civil society, and issues relating to the military, foreign policy and China's soft power. He then considers how far the Third Plenum actually went in addressing them.

China at the Crossroads: the Third Plenum and China's Reform Challenges

David Shambaugh

Ambassador Browne, Mr Deputy Vice-Chancellor, Minister Groser, and particularly Acting Director Peter Harris, who I would like to thank for the invitation. I'm glad to be here and to address the topic of China at the crossroads.

It's a very, very timely topic. For China watchers China always seems to be at the crossroads. But what is different this time is that we can assess this question in the context of the Third Plenum held late last year. And we have a very stimulating day ahead of us with a number of really leading international experts, China experts who have travelled both from within New Zealand and from overseas to address a variety of the more refined aspects of the Third Plenum decisions last year.

The Third Plenum last year came thirty-five years, as I'm sure you know, after Deng Xiaoping launched China's reforms in 1978 at another Third Plenum, the Third Plenum of the Eleventh Central Committee – last November it was the Third Plenum of the Eighteenth Central Committee. The previous Third Plenum, of course, set China on the path to what it has become today. This has been a very successful journey, unprecedented in world history in the magnitude of what has been accomplished on a variety of levels.

Indeed it is truly impressive. But a number of China watchers outside China, as well as many Chinese that I have talked to inside China – Chinese intellectuals that is – have judged that the nation really has reached a crossroads at the present time, and is facing a series of critical junctures in the economic, social, political, environmental, intellectual, foreign policy and national security domains, as well as in other areas of development. And these observers all agree on one thing: that the nation has reached diminishing returns with the old growth model that Deng Xiaoping set in train thirty-five years ago, and that the main elements of that broad reform programme from the first Third Plenum are no longer as applicable and sustainable for China's future continued economic, social and other forms of development as they once were. Indeed China's own leaders, particularly former Premier Wen Jiabao, have used the term 'unsustainable' to describe a number of policy areas in China.

Mr Peter Harris, Acting Director of the New Zealand Contemporary China Research Centre, introducing the keynote speaker

Many China watchers, foreign China watchers at least, believe that a kind of tipping point has been reached in contemporary China's development on multiple fronts, and that unless fundamental changes are undertaken, national growth will stagnate. So don't count, Mr Minister, on the kind of trajectory you have seen in the last three decades.

These foreign China watchers not only believe that there is a tipping point possible but that even the entire political system could come apart in China and that China could be entering, or has already entered, the 'middle income trap' and a period of long stagnation. (Stagnation with Chinese characteristics, perhaps: this is not a Japanese-style stagnation, but a stagnation that might still have 5–6 per cent growth, albeit with massaged statistics.) In the United States there is consensus amongst China watchers that the party-state in China is in serious trouble on a number of fronts and that we should not blindly assume its longevity. Professor Kerry Brown, who will speak next, is going to address some of these issues. So I personally share the perspective that China does face daunting challenges, and that China is indeed at a crossroads – that the title of your conference is quite apt.

What I would like to do to elaborate that perspective is to identify ten key policy challenges that I see China facing today. Then I am going to take a few minutes to assess how the Third Plenum addresses or does not address those ten challenges.

The first policy challenge is indeed in the economic domain, and in re-orientating the macro-economic growth model that Deng Xiaoping launched thirty-five years ago – a model that had two main elements to it, domestic capital investment plus exports – towards a new model based on domestic consumption and building a knowledge economy. So two old elements are trying to find two new elements. There are also other critical economic elements, most notably spurring innovation as a means of becoming a knowledge economy, and reforming SOEs (state owned enterprises) so as to lessen if not break the monopoly stranglehold SOEs now have on various sectors of the Chinese economy. Those of you who studied Marxism in university will recall Lenin's thesis of almost a hundred years ago, *Imperialism, the Highest Stage of Capitalism*, in which he identified the phenomenon of 'state monopoly capitalism' (*guojia longduan zibenzhuyi* 国家垄断资本主义 in Chinese). Well, I would submit that that is exactly what China has today – state monopoly capitalism.

Other economic elements that we will hear about today are *hukou* 户口 (household registration) restrictions and the effects that they are having. *Hukou* is the residency system in China that prevents people, at least legally, from moving around and taking residence, drawing on public services, and working in places other than the place where they are granted their *hukou*. This has placed great impediments on creating a true national labour market. Financial sector reform is also needed – a variety of issues there – as is the further opening of the Chinese economy to the outside world.

So while we all admire the economic accomplishments of China over the last three decades, many believe that fundamental and qualitative changes are needed if the country is going to continue to develop, at least at the same pace, over the next three decades. So that's the first cluster of issues – economic ones.

The second cluster of issues are social ones – reducing social instabilities and inequalities. I'm sure you are familiar with the measure called the Gini coefficient, which measures income inequalities in societies. China today has one of the world's highest Gini coefficients, almost 0.5, and you could have a slide similar to the one shown earlier by Minister Groser on how Gini coefficient data have moved over the last few years – it would be quite dramatic. So China is a highly unequal society today with little trickle-down in income. The middle class has grown, but has now begun to stagnate in terms of income. As for the upper class, if you will, those that have become quite wealthy – today China has the world's largest number of millionaires and the world's second largest number of billionaires – you have to ask where they are putting their money, their personal assets. The answer is: overseas, not at home. They have their bank accounts overseas, they have their children overseas, they have their relatives overseas, they buy property overseas. And that is a telling indicator. It's a telling indicator when a country's elite, its economic elite, have one foot out the door and are ready to move the other foot out the door when things get shaky.

Professor David Shambaugh from George Washington University talking about the Third Plenum

There are rising frustrations, really, throughout Chinese society. I have been going to China every year for thirty-five consecutive years, and I have never sensed the kinds of tensions and frustrations that I do in China today. In talking to virtually everyone I find that it's a highly frustrated society, and these frustrations are boiling over. They are boiling over into two hundred thousand reported protests per year – these are official figures, so in reality probably much higher – and indeed, as we know and read, ethnic unrest and acts of terrorism are spiking in Xinjiang (in northwest China), and in Tibet. So on the social front I find

China to be a highly frustrated society in all sectors, and indeed a country with significant instability.

The third challenge area is combatting corruption, which is endemic and systemic in the Chinese Communist Party, in the state, in the military and indeed throughout society – costing the economy untold billions, compromising the Party's legitimacy, and compromising military effectiveness and competence. We had a development in that last area just the day before yesterday, with the arrest and expulsion from the Communist Party of General Xu Caihou, former Vice-Chairman of the Central Military Commission. That's high ranking. He's the highest ranking military official to be removed from office since Lin Biao apparently tried to assassinate Chairman Mao in 1971 and crashed in an airplane in Mongolia.

Corruption is widespread, endemic, systemic. It's not a new problem for China but it has truly reached epidemic proportions. In response the Xi Jinping administration has launched an unprecedented anti-corruption campaign under the leadership of Wang Qishan, a Politburo Member, and President Xi has said this campaign aims to capture both 'tigers and flies' (high-ranking officials and low-ranking party members). So far there have just been a lot of flies, with a few mosquitoes and birds, so to speak, but Xu Caihao – he's a tiger. The day before yesterday the Party Secretary of Guangzhou was also detained for Party corruption investigation – he's a tiger too. And of course all eyes are on the man named Zhou Yongkang, a former Politburo Member, retired now, and the head of China's pervasive security apparatus. Many of Zhou's clients, if you will, or people in his network, have already been taken down, and the big question now is whether Party leaders are willing to indict Zhou Yongkang as well.

So this is a pretty serious campaign. But I would remind you that when Jiang Zemin became the Party leader and when Hu Jintao became the Party leader, they both started off their tenure with very aggressive anti-corruption campaigns. These lasted about eighteen months each. We are almost at that point now with the Xi Jinping campaign. This one seems more serious; let's hope it is. It better be, because the corruption situation is extremely serious and any student of modern Chinese history knows that the previous two regimes, if you will – the Republican Nationalist government and the Qing government – fell for a variety of reasons but amongst those reasons was corruption.

So that's the third challenge. But the problem is not just about attacking corruption, but how far to go. It's like pulling a ball of yarn or string. Once you start unravelling the problem, it unravels rather quickly and can go to places that you don't predict. There have been reports in the Hong Kong media in the last few days, in fact, that Jiang Zemin, the former President, has weighed in and effectively said to Xi Jinping, 'Enough is enough – don't go any further'. Why? Because many of the people implicated in current corruption investigations are tied to Jiang Zemin himself, and were put into power by him or were promoted or benefited in their careers during his tenure. So how far do you pull that ball of string? It's a tough question. So we'll see how it plays out.

The fourth challenge is undertaking political and legal reform. This is direly needed, not just for political reasons or social reasons, but for economic reasons. There is a real need to facilitate innovation in society in order to build a knowledge economy and to become really globally competitive in inventive areas, and to move from China being an assembly and processor economy, which it has always been and is still, to a creative economy. Politics and the political system, the educational system and the legal system are all intricately bound up with the innovation question.

But political reforms are needed not only to facilitate innovation in the next stage of economic growth but also to control corruption, protect citizens' rights and give a voice to the aspirations and indeed the complaints of average citizens. None of this can occur without the loosening of the political system, which in fact is getting tighter and tighter. Just the opposite to a loosening has been happening under Xi Jinping and indeed happened during the second five years of his predecessor Hu Jintao. We are now into year five of an unprecedented crackdown – unprecedented that is since the June 4th 1989 crackdown – by the security authorities on various sectors of Chinese society and on information, internal dissent, NGOs (non-governmental organisations), and other forms of political activism.

Since last year this crackdown has been extremely severe. Xi Jinping launched it and various other Politburo Members are associated with it. They have issued a number of orders, the so-called Seven No's, the Six Why's, the mass line campaign and most draconian of all, Central Document No 9 (2013). All of these reveal a really paranoid party-state, fearing subversion from the West and particularly the United States. So political repression – repression coming in a number of different ways, including information repression – is I would judge the worst it has been for twenty-five years, since June 4th 1989.

And having just flown here from Beijing where I spent much of the last week, I can tell you it has many manifestations – not the least of which is getting online. Google, the world's largest internet firm, and Gmail are both blocked – you can't even access email. They want to build a knowledge economy and they block the world's largest internet firm – how is that going to help their drive for innovation?

The fifth big challenge area is urbanisation. This is a particular pet project of Premier Li Keqiang. The goal is to have 60 per cent of the population living in urban areas ('urban' meaning 'extended municipal') by 2020. This means relocating an additional 260 million people – think about that for a second, that is about the size of the United States – moving 260 million rural inhabitants to urban areas by 2020, creating 110 million new jobs for them in urban areas, and absorbing rural migrants and providing them with legitimate rights to education, healthcare and other public services. This is an enormous undertaking to carry out in six years. It boggles the mind even thinking of those numbers. No government on the face of the planet has ever attempted it, so that in itself is going to be the fifth major challenge.

The sixth big challenge is improving the environment. All of us who have been to China know that it has the world's worst, not just in air pollution but in water resources, lead deposits in rivers causing life-threatening cancer, desertification, deforestation, climate change, inefficient energy use and so on, all of these directly affecting human health, economic growth and indeed the planet's global warming. It is also, I would add, a potentially volatile political issue. Mainland China need look no further than across the Taiwan Strait to see how democracy got started on the island of Taiwan – it started with something called the Lukang rebellion over the building of a nuclear power plant in southern Taiwan several decades ago. So environmental issues are very political, and we have seen citizens organise across the country on this issue.

The seventh big issue is empowering civil society. This too is not just a political issue but a social issue, because as all societies modernise citizen organisation and activism increases. In political science we call this 'interest aggregation and articulation'. It's both a vertical process by which society organises its interests and articulates them to the state, and a horizontal process whereby the local state can partner with NGOs to address a range of community problems. This also involves a transmission of information within society. China not only has a very underdeveloped civil society; in my opinion the party-state needs to keep it this way, working very hard to retard, not stimulate, the growth of civil society because it's deathly afraid of a bottom-up political movement that will threaten the regime. So this is another cluster of issues.

Let me just tick off the last three and then note the extent to which the Third Plenum addresses these ten issues.

The eighth challenge is the need, or the attempt, to build international soft power. As China has become a global power, it has become increasingly concerned with its international image, which is not particularly good. In fact, if you look at the major public opinion polls done annually by the Pew Global Attitudes Survey, we have seen a secular decline of China's image by nearly twenty points worldwide since 2007. So China's image is deteriorating on a global basis and it is mixed to poor almost everywhere – actually not everywhere, in fact, as there are some pockets in Africa, Southeast Asia, Pakistan, a few other countries, and maybe New Zealand, in which it is more positive. But overall China's image is suffering abroad, and this is no secret.

It's no secret to the Chinese government, who are pouring billions of dollars, approximately $12–15 billion per year, into a variety of mechanisms to try and improve China's voice, get China's voice heard in the international media, improve its image, and transmit Chinese values – and indeed the Chinese language, through Confucius Institutes and other mechanisms. So China is trying, with a policy the government decided on in 2008 and has invested in in the years since then. So far it is too early to say whether the investment is paying off. We don't know and won't know for a few years yet whether this is the case. But so far it doesn't seem to be.

Thus far China's soft power is not resonating abroad. China is not a magnet that is attracting others to it, which in essence is soft power – if you have soft power others want to emulate you, want to be like you, want to do things your way. The fact is, there are not a lot of countries in the world queuing up to do things the Chinese way. Why? Because the Chinese way is sui generis in all spheres, including economic development. It isn't easily exported, it isn't easily replicable in other societies. That too is the essence of soft power. If you have soft power you have universality, your values travel, your methods travel, your systems travel, it's like a magnetic effect where others want to be like you. Well, so far there aren't many – if any – countries in the world that seem to want to be like China. So that's a big challenge for the government.

The ninth challenge is improving the country's military combat effectiveness. The PLA, the People's Liberation Army, has come a very long way in the last two decades, and not only in its hardware. But it still has a number of what you might call software problems in the areas of logistics, command and control, information, 'combined arms' readiness and power projection. China has no power projection beyond its immediate periphery. Maybe it can project power a few hundred nautical miles, out perhaps to the first island chain along the West Pacific rim – but not beyond that. China could not project power down here to New Zealand if it wanted to; it just doesn't have the capacity – naval, air or otherwise. Missiles, yes – it could land a missile here in this room if it wanted to, but that's a pretty blunt instrument. So the PLA has come a long way, as I say, but it has a lot of integrative software problems still to solve – some of which the Third Plenum does in fact address.

The last challenge that we need to recognise is managing strained foreign relations. Overall I would say that China's foreign relations are strained everywhere in the world – with a few exceptions, the exceptions being Russia, Central Asia, parts of Africa, the Caribbean states, Cambodia, Laos, Venezuela, Cuba, Pakistan – and perhaps New Zealand (seriously!). So there are some pockets of favourability and in those countries China has a more positive image and its foreign relations are, on balance, really quite good. But everywhere else, throughout Asia, throughout Europe, increasingly in Latin America, increasingly even in Africa, and certainly in the United States, we see China's diplomacy encountering difficulties, with most countries having a number of points of friction with China, and China acting in a more assertive, tough, uncompromising and nationalistic way. We are dealing with a different China today; the stronger it has become, the tougher, more nationalistic, more assertive and more difficult it is to deal with. We see this in the East China Sea, in the South China Sea, in the border with India, and in relations with a number of other countries, including the United States. As far as Sino-American relations go, we are experiencing really considerable tensions and difficulties in the relationship, with deepening strategic mistrust, rising strategic competition and frictions in virtually every policy sphere. And one must recognise, I think, that this is to be expected. It is predictable and natural for rising powers and established powers to have such frictions and strategic mistrust. We are going to hear more on this from Marc Lanteigne in his presentation.

Professor David Shambaugh and part of the audience

So these are the ten big challenges that I see confronting China today. In the brief time left let me try and see if I can marry these challenges to the Third Plenum documents. There are three documents in fact: the Communiqué, the Decision, and the Explanation that Xi Jinping issued on how to interpret and read the other two documents. The Decision is the main document. It contains 22,000 Chinese characters and identifies more than three hundred special reforms in sixty different categories. Impressive, very impressive. But if you read the Decision and the other documents, the Communiqué in particular, you are struck overall by the odd mixture of ambition and caution in them. The reformist rhetoric, and indeed there is a lot of reformist rhetoric in them, is indeed encouraging, as China does definitely need a bold new vision and bold new leadership in this juncture of its development. But in many places the document is also very vague in its wording and lacking in specificity. This vagueness or opacity suggests to me – and indeed has been put to me by many Chinese I have asked about it – that there is a lack of determination and an irresolution of policy on certain issues, with continuing debate behind the scenes and anticipated bureaucratic resistance to the reforms.

Nonetheless, if you read the documents all together they are an impressive attempt to grapple with a full and complex agenda of issues. And they do offer encouraging signs of reform. In fact, I am a little more positive about these documents now than when I wrote an earlier analysis of them right after the Plenum concluded. I have re-read them now several times – you really have to read and re-read them, and read them carefully to try and get to the bottom of what they are saying – so I am a bit more positive about them than before, and believe they do offer a number of new reforms.

The most immediately evident are the loosening of the 'one child' policy; the abolition of the 'reform through labour' system; an enhanced role for the market in determining resource allocation; making government budgets more transparent; more fully funding public welfare expenditures; and creating some new bureaucratic mechanisms at the top of the system, such as the State Security Commission and the Leading Group on Comprehensively Deepening Reforms, with hints about a new super environmental agency. So there are encouraging statements and initiatives in these areas.

There are also suggestions that there will be new reforms in the financial and banking sectors, and movement towards renminbi capital account convertibility. (Professor Christine Wong will speak to the financial issues in her presentation). There are suggestions about an improved foreign investment climate in China. The new pilot free-trade zone in Shanghai is discussed. Enhancement of property rights is discussed at some length (and Professor Jonathan Unger from the Australian National University will be addressing that issue later today). There is also talk about improving the tax system, about enhancing the People's Congresses and so-called 'consultative democracy' – which I have to put into quotation marks – and about judicial and legal reform, with some intriguing language with respect to that last issue.

So there is indeed potential in these areas for real innovation and policy breakthroughs. But the devil is going to be in the detail, and unfortunately these documents provide very few details about how their stated goals will be achieved. So implementation has to be awaited. And one thing we can anticipate for sure is significant bureaucratic resistance. In fact we have already seen this in the SOE sector in particular. Even the low-hanging fruit, you might say, are not so easy to pick, and we have to anticipate that the Plenum decisions are going to be resisted. But this is natural. Whenever you try and break rice bowls and move a nation on to a new path, away from the one it's become very comfortable with, it's a very difficult thing to do. So the regime is already getting pushback and resistance.

An interesting new project that I've just learnt about and want to alert you to is the assessment of how Third Plenum decisions are being implemented that the Asia Society in the United States is about to start publishing every quarter.

So let me conclude and sum up. Only time will tell if this most recent Third Plenum turns out to be a watershed like the famous Third Plenum in 1978. I suspect that the proverbial glass of water will be half full or half empty, depending on how it's viewed. The results are going to be mixed, in some areas successful, in other areas not. Certainly China's leaders are to be commended for putting together such a comprehensive document, and trying to identify in such a comprehensive fashion the challenges that they confront. That's the first step to addressing them successfully. Many of the challenges are interlinked, and there is evidence that they have begun to think about the linkages among policy areas rather than simply addressing them in a piecemeal fashion.

But, as I say, the devil is going to be in the details of implementation. There is sure to be a lot of resistance. China may not be a democracy but it certainly has entrenched interest groups in a variety of sectors, not the least of which – and this is one point I do want to make – is the Chinese Communist Party itself. One can observe from world history that it is not very common for those that have wealth, power and privilege to divest them voluntarily in the broader interests of the nation, and I would suggest the Chinese Communist Party is not about to do so either. So the question I want to leave with you, the question many China watchers are indeed asking themselves, is whether the Chinese Communist Party itself is not now the greatest impediment to further reform. Party leaders facilitated the last three decades of reform, but now they are into new territory where the Party and the political system may be an impediment to further economic and social reform. So let me leave you with that intriguing possibility. Anyway, China is at a crossroads domestically and in terms of its foreign relations and will continue to be an interesting story for all of us to follow.

Thank you very much for your attention. I look forward to my colleagues' presentations. We have a very rich day ahead of us, and I think we all stand to learn a lot – so thank you very much.

Panel 1: (from left) Professor Kerry Brown from the University of Sydney, Professor Jonathan Unger from the Australian National University (ANU), Professor Anita Chan from the University of Technology, Sydney, and Dr Stephen Noakes from the University of Auckland

Part of the audience

PART ONE
GOVERNANCE AND SOCIETY

China is pervaded by corrupt practices, often involving officials. President Xi Jinping has made a concerted campaign against corruption a cornerstone – some say the cornerstone – of his administration. The campaign has spread wider and deeper than anyone anticipated, and has struck at unprecedentedly high levels of the Party and the state, most recently with the announcement of an investigation into what amount to corruption charges of Zhou Yongkang, the most senior Communist leader ever to have faced such charges. Professor Kerry Brown considers what President Xi's underlying motives in conducting the campaign are, and how the campaign may be part of the Communist Party of China's efforts to portray itself as the historical and ethical driving force behind China's resurgence.

The Moral Basis of Party Rule under Xi Jinping, and the Party's Search for a System of Ethics in the Twenty-First Century

Kerry Brown

About thirty years ago in Fujian province, a young official who had just arrived there made a comment to the local Xinhua news agency, saying that if you wanted to make money you should not go into politics. This was a radical statement in contemporary China, and the young official did in fact go on to try and get into the Communist Party Central Committee in 1997, when he got the lowest number of votes. But in 2007 he was brought to the centre anyway with the patronage of a number of different elite leaders including Zeng Jinghong and Jiang Zemin; and today he is the President of China, Mr Xi Jinping.

Well, I suppose that was an interesting thing for a politician to say thirty years ago, especially in Fujian, which even early on was undergoing pretty dynamic economic changes, being very innovative in engaging with what is categorised as overseas investment. But I suppose we can see a distinctive mindset even then in this young official; and now he is the person we are trying to understand every day of our lives.

Xi Jinping has been called a strong man, he has been called a new Mao, in a new book published by Yu Jie he has been called China's godfather. In fact the book even has a picture of him, strangely, sitting next to Marlon Brando . . . though I don't think the two of them met.

The chair of panel 1, Professor Anne-Marie Brady from the University of Canterbury

So I am interested in what narrative we give President Xi, and what he believes, and what he believes about the Chinese Communist Party's ethical basis. It is a strange thing after all to talk about the ethical basis of the Party. The Third Plenum document that we are talking about – the Plenum Decision – does in its first and second paragraphs talk of value systems. It says that the Party needs to establish and develop socialism with Chinese characteristics, to guarantee socialist modernisation. In the second paragraph it goes on to say that the Party needs to uphold the great banner of socialism with Chinese characteristics, to support the socialist market economy, and put promotion of social fairness, justice and improvement of people's lives first. Then finally it comes to the idea of reform being centred on building the core socialist values and a system of developing a socialist culture.

According to the book by Yu Jie, the particular values that Xi Jinping believes in are in fact from his time in Yan'an in Shaanxi province when he was part of a Red Guard group, not a formal one but a kind of late 1960s–early 1970s small revolutionary band, in which (he said himself later, in the late 1990s) he imbibed the values of the Yan'an spirit – the spirit of idealism, the spirit of conviction, the spirit of the Party having a moral basis.

But the book by Yu Jie, which has been banned in China – in fact one of the editors who originally put it out was I think imprisoned in Shenzhen only early this year – this very controversial book whose author now lives in America claims that the issue at the heart of the Communist Party's crisis of faith, and it has been a long

Professor Kerry Brown talking about corruption and Communist Party ethics

crisis of faith now, the issue at the heart of Xi Jinping and his particular belief system and those of his colleagues around him is that the sole consistent and coherent body of ideas that they really had profound exposure to when they were young was Mao Zedong Thought. So we can say that they are Maoists, only in the sense that when they were nurtured, when they were young, when they were really getting on their ideological feet, as it were, Maoism was the only game in town. And it has been a hard thing for them to lose hold of.

And the problem as Yu Jie goes on to analyse it in his book is that Maoism has a kind of extraordinary privileging of the institutions and the forces of power. It is, almost as George Orwell said, a Party built on the image of the strong hand, of the strong force basically forcing everyone else to do what it says. What's that got to do therefore with ethics, with the softer things that the Plenum talks about, of the new culture of modernisation and of Party faith?

Well, I suppose you can say that the Plenum document in some senses is also a political critique. It is a critique of the do-nothing era of Hu Jintao, of the *wu wei* (无为, do nothing) period as we call it – that extraordinary moment when China grew more and more powerful, more and more wealthy, and yet in terms of its own intrinsic, inner nature, its existential nature, it did nothing. In one critique issued in Hong Kong, then President Hu Jintao was accused of failing from 2008 on to deal with the core political and economic deliverables of stability in Tibet, stability in Xinjiang, stability in Inner Mongolia in 2011. He saw an extraordinary increase of social protest, an extraordinary period of a renaissance of contention in Chinese society, and a kind of fractiousness in society, something that David has just referred to, a frustrated China, a China that was rich but did not know what it believed.

Last month in Denmark I was part of a small group of people who met the man in charge of the ideology of the Party, Liu Yunshan, who is the number five in the Politburo. Liu Yunshan is in fact the only journalist to have become a Member of the Standing Committee of the Politburo (the Chinese Party's top ruling group). He was the livestock and grain correspondent for Xinhua in Inner Mongolia in the early 1980s. You don't get sexier job titles than that, do you?

Liu is the only one of the seven members of the Standing Committee of the Politburo who hasn't had senior-level experience as a provincial Party Secretary. He has had a career wholly in the ideology or thought management apparatus, and so he is an important person to listen to. He is the odd man out, and he is the odd man out because in a sense for these issues of values, of the ethical basis of what the Party believes in, the things about its own internal nature and belief systems, he is the person who somehow has to come up with the answers.

The one thing he did say in our small seminar was that the Party is the expression of all Chinese people's political ideals. I know it's been said before by other elite leaders over the last thirty years, but this was a very bold, a pretty daring thing for someone in his position at this time to say. He said the Communist Party of China was the recipient, the beneficiary of five thousand years of traditional Chinese culture, and was therefore not just a political expression, but also a cultural expression and an expression of ideas.

For those who have seen the Party in operation and the way in which it enforces and implements particular policies, this is a startling idea. Perhaps the most forensic critique of the Party's moral activity and its own particular internal belief systems is that by Liu Xiaobo, the Nobel Laureate who of course is now in prison for the pains he took in trying to describe what he called the inner lives of Party cadres in the twenty-first century. For him, as you'll see in his book (published in English translation a couple of years ago), the issue really is that the Party doesn't have a moral basis for its behaviour, but is purely about the monetarisation of power and power structures, and that this is therefore an extraordinary moral evacuation and moral traitorism or treachery, a betrayal of the Party's founding values in 1949 as the bringer of justice and a new political narrative to the People's Republic of China after decades of oppression, war and conflict.

It's obvious therefore, it seems to me, that when we look underneath all the economic and policy rhetoric of the Plenum document, we are seeing a Party institution which is reappraising its role in society, and is therefore at a crossroads. Does it dare to claim a greater role, does it dare to go for a bigger space, does it dare to say, as Liu Yunshan said last month, that it is not a political party in the way we know it but a social force, something bigger, that it almost has a holistic role in society, a unique and extraordinary function, and is utterly at the centre of China's project of modernity? This search for legitimacy is not just a search, as Hu Jintao said, for more GDP growth or delivering absolute tangible economic outcomes; it is also a search for new and complicated forms of legitimacy in cultural and moral areas.

I think the crisis really is that on one hand we have the rhetorical structures of Marxism-Leninism, which are spelt out in the Plenum document and ones that we all know well, while on the other hand we have this imperative to modernisation. And that therefore the language of Marxism-Leninism, with its particular privileging of power and sometimes force, is being tempered by the need to have more complicated outcomes and modernisation of the very values of which the Party is built up.

I think at the heart of that is the fact that until recent years the Party has been thoroughly utilitarian in its ethical system. The ends have justified the means. If you look at the way the Party explained its history, in the documents produced only a couple of years ago by the Central Committee, it talked about how, you know, we have been through many experiences, we have been through the three great periods of building our legitimacy through foreign war, through unifying the country and through reform and opening up from 1978 on, but the issue really is that we are the bastion of modernity in China, and that no matter what happened, even if it was the Great Leap Forward or the Cultural Revolution, despite all these things, it was okay, we justified what we did, we managed to survive because what we were doing was right. The ends did justify the means.

A couple of years ago there was an interesting discussion about former Premier Wen Jiabao reading Adam Smith. It was interesting because he wasn't reportedly reading *The Wealth of Nations* but a lesser known book by Adam Smith, *The Theory of Moral Sentiments*. When you actually look at *The Theory of Moral Sentiments*, it is an extraordinary book for us even to claim that a Politburo member could be reading. This is because the fundamental argument in Smith's book is that economic and structural issues are not the only thing; humans have to listen to the inner man as well. The inner man, he said, is the voice of conscience, of our inner sentiments of rightness or wrongness, the thing that makes us different; we are not just animals in the natural world – we have an instinct to form moral consciousness.

So finally I'd like to ask, how do we place this whole kind of thinking about the moral behaviour of the Party with its complex utilitarian past, this new desire to have something richer at a time when China is undergoing numerous social and moral crises? What are we to try and make of it?

One resource that the Party does have to hand is the rich heritage of ethical thinking in China's past. There have already been raids on, for instance, the Confucian legacy, and others of the great pre-Qin era thinkers, with varying levels of conviction. The idea that the Communist Party's unique role in contemporary Chinese society, its political dominance and its self-postulated intimate link with the national mission to be a great and powerful country, legitimises this sort of move on classical thinking and the use of ideas from the ancient dynastic era to supply at least some sort of ethical framework today can be evidenced, for instance, in the use of 'taking people as the key', which was first mooted by Hu Jintao but has subsequently been used by other major leaders.

It seems to me that there is an issue about the anti-corruption campaign at the moment, which is the struggle for this moral formation. It is, we could say, almost an epic or a tragic struggle. It involves the kinds of issues that have been talked about already, particular figures suffering or being felled, that's true. But we would be misinterpreting it, I think, if we just saw it – as Yu Jie's book and a number of other analyses do – as a kind of strongman politics, of someone trying to wage a single war so as to have more powers, as some interpreters see Xi Jinping as doing. I think we would misunderstand it if we saw it just as that.

This anti-corruption campaign seems to me to be an interesting new kind of purge, because it is not actually about what people are doing, but what they are believing. Anyone in the elite could be banged up today for being venal and greedy, because all of them are connected to networks of extraordinary wealth formation. So it seems to me that if we look hard at the people who have been taken in, there is something about what they believe, something about what they feel the role of the Party is. There is a profoundly ideological bent to this anti-corruption campaign. This is actually a long-term issue. It is not just something that Xi Jinping has alerted the Party to. And it isn't something that'll be easy for us to engage with and understand.

In the very final years of the Hu Jintao period, Hu made a speech in which, for a man we know is not the world's most expressive individual, he sounded almost lyrically lamenting. He said that we must beware of the Party not being able to satisfy people's deeper expectations. And he used a phrase: one day if we are not careful all the things we have could be taken from us. It seems to me therefore that at the heart of all the economic, structural and institutional issues that the Plenum document talks about, there is this issue finally of what the seven people in the Politburo Standing Committee believe, what is in their hearts, what their inner worlds are driven by.

Dealing with the ownership of land, especially rural land, has been a vexed question in China ever since Deng Xiaoping's reforms began thirty-five years ago. In the countryside China still retains in name the collective system of land ownership first introduced in the 1950s, although in the reform era land-use rights have often been contracted out to individual farming households. In recent years the unjust requisitioning of collectively-owned rural land by local governments so that they can develop the land more profitably has become a major bone of contention, and sometimes the cause of local unrest. Some people expected the Third Plenum to introduce some form of land privatisation as a means of dealing with both the requisition issue and the issue of how to achieve economies of scale in the countryside as the rural population moves gradually into urbanised areas. Professor Jonathan Unger explains why, in his view, the Plenum's failure to privatise rural land was in fact a positive decision.

The Third Plenum and Rural Property Rights: Decisions in the Right Direction

Jonathan Unger

In the lead up to the Third Plenum, rumours swirled in China and among China specialists abroad that China's rural landholdings were going to be privatised into the hands of individual farmers. It was even claimed that the Prime Minister, Li Keqiang, had approvingly hinted at this at a forum a month or so before the Plenum. Chinese economists who had been trained in the West had long advocated this, using the mantra 'farmers need secure property rights' to argue that farmland should be converted into farmers' private property.

In the event, the Plenum announced the opposite, declaring 'We will maintain the collective ownership of land' (Plenum Decision, Article 20) and 'We will safeguard the rights and interests of farmers as members of collective economic organizations' (Article 21).[1] These firm announcements came as a surprise to many.

I presume that some economists feel the Plenum's decision was erroneous. Contrarily, I am convinced the Chinese leadership made the right decision, and I feel relieved by it.

Let me explain the context. During the period of Mao's rule, the land was farmed collectively. At that time, 15–50 neighbouring families were members of a so-

---

1 The official English-language translation of the Third Plenum's Decision can be found at http://www.china.org.cn/china/third_plenary_session/2014-01/16/content_31212602.htm. The original Chinese-language version is at http://news.xinhuanet.com/politics/2013-11/15/c_118164235.htm

called production team. They owned a stretch of fields as a group, worked the land together, and divided up the harvest yields in kind and cash each year based on how much labour each family had contributed. Subsequently, during the early 1980s, in the early years of Deng Xiaoping's rule, the land was divided up among families to farm independently. This was normally done on a per capita basis. That is, a family that had six members received six shares of land, a family with three members three shares of land.[2] But they did not receive legal ownership of this land. The former production teams, which today are called villager small groups, have continued to own the agricultural land collectively, while their member families hold a right to cultivate the collective land apportioned to them on thirty-year contracts without any rental charge. Surveys in China have shown that most farmers have preferred this system rather than a system of private land ownership. For example, a 2004 survey by Chinese researchers of 306 farm families spread across forty rural counties in Anhui province found that 71 per cent of the respondents favoured retaining what the Chinese author referred to as 'land cooperatives', while only 7 per cent opposed this.[3]

One salient reason is that the decollectivisation of agriculture and the return to family farming created a dilemma for many farming households. As time passed they found they faced a shortage of land, as children were born and as their family grew. They and fellow 'villager small group' members turned to an unusual solution. I headed a research project that carried out a questionnaire survey in 2008 of 476 villager small groups spread across 57 of Anhui province's rural counties.[4] Disregarding the thirty-year household contracts stipulated by the national government, the survey revealed that fully 95 per cent of all the villager small groups had reallocated the land among families at least once since 1984. Even more striking, about 75 per cent of these land distributions were carried out explicitly and only in order to re-equalise landholdings on a per capita basis. This was in

---

2 Jonathan Unger, 'The Decollectivization of the Chinese Countryside: A Survey of Twenty-eight Villages', *Pacific Affairs* 58, no. 4 (Winter 1985): 585–606.
3 'Nongmin dui nongdi zhidu gaige de renzhi—jiyu Anhui sheng nonghu diaocha ziliao fenxi' ('Farmers' Sense of the Agricultural Land System Reforms—Analysing the Materials from a Survey of Anhui Province Farm Households'), *Zhongguo nongcun jingji* 中国农村经济 (Chinese Rural Economy), no. 7 (2005), p. 46. Similarly, in a 1994 questionnaire survey of 800 farm families in eight counties spread across China, only 14 per cent of the respondents declared they preferred permanent land ownership rights to be held by each household. Fully 65 per cent favoured periodic land reallocations to redistribute plots to families that had grown in size, and only 19 per cent were opposed. James Kung and Shouying Liu, 'Farmers' Preferences Regarding Ownership and Land Tenure in Post-Mao China: Unexpected Evidence from Eight Counties', *The China Journal*, no. 38 (July 1997), pp. 45–48.
4 The results of this survey are discussed in detail in Sherry Tao Kong and Jonathan Unger, 'Egalitarian Redistributions of Agricultural Land in China through Community Consensus: Findings from Two Surveys', *The China Journal*, no. 69 (January 2013), pp. 1–19. Dr Graeme Smith played a vital role in the design and organisation of the survey.

order to provide extra land for families that had expanded in size through births or weddings (with brides marrying into families), while families that had decreased in size through deaths and the departure of daughters into marriage lost land. Most of the families wanted this system as a household strategy to balance out the economic stresses of the family cycle. A vote almost always was taken among small group members before a land reallocation, and usually three quarters of the households needed to approve. In doing this, they have been bucking the Chinese government, which opposes such land reallocations and passed a strong directive in 1993 banning them and then increasingly strong laws in 1998 and 2003 that outlawed them. Nevertheless, the land redistributions quietly continued.

The Third Plenum's Decision yet again declares 'we will . . . protect farmers' contracted land-use rights . . . which will remain unchanged for a long time to come' (Article 20). In other words it again stresses that land redistributions are banned. However, since two top-level directives (*zhongfa* 中发) and a law have already been in place between 1993 and 2003 banning land reallocations, and since villager small groups across China have ignored the national law, this new Plenum declaration, which does not even have the force of law, cannot be expected to have any effect.

In any case, the numbers of such land reallocations have been in gradual decline anyway due to major changes in the rural economy. In particular, as all of us know, high numbers of villagers have been leaving the countryside to take up work in factories that produce most of what we wear today and much of the goods we buy in shops. In many villages, this means a lower dependence on agriculture, and separately, with more labour away and less labour available in villages, it also means less population pressure on the land.[5] In most of rural China, there is no longer any need to reallocate land in order to survive in a type of agriculture that until two decades ago was largely equivalent to subsistence farming. As a result, in the dozen years between 1996 and 2008 only 33 per cent of the villager small groups in our survey reallocated land for household-demographic reasons, down considerably from approximately 90 per cent of the villager small groups which had done so in the previous dozen years.

Does this precipitous decline mean that the farmers' land reallocations will gradually peter out of their own accord? That is not likely. In the survey, 85 per cent of the villager small group heads (who are farmers elected to their posts) declared support for continuing to carry out land redistributions in the future.

When asked why, some commented that they see this as a matter of promises and

---

5   A survey study that analysed land reallocation behaviour in ten provinces in China for the period 1986–1999 similarly found that where a large share of the able-bodied were engaged in off-farm work, the overall level of land reallocation dropped sharply over time. (James K. Kung, Justin Y. Lin, and Shen Minggao, 'Structural Change and the Evolution of Property Rights in Rural China', unpublished paper manuscript.) A similar finding appears in Scott Rozelle and Guo Li, 'Village Leaders and Land-Rights Formation in China', *The American Economic Review*, Vol. 88, no. 2 (1998), p. 437.

fairness and explained that some villagers had given up land in previous reallocations in the expectation that as their own family conditions changed they would regain land during a future reallocation. Others answered that the long-term or permanent departure to the cities of migrant workers upsets the land balance within the villager small group, leaving some land under-utilised until a new redistribution occurs. Others saw the collective land system as a safeguard against farm families being dispossessed of their land due to debts (as has occurred in many other developing countries). Other interviewees viewed future land redistributions as a safety net for migrant workers who settle in cities but might in future lose their urban jobs, either for personal reasons or because of an economic recession. As one small-group head explained, 'In our small group, we've never had a case of anyone who's gone out and then came back and didn't get a share of land'.

Professor Jonathan Unger talking about rural land ownership

A system of collective land also strengthens farmers' capacity to resist land requisitions by local governments. In rural areas near cities or where industrialisation is expanding, it has been common for local governments to confiscate agricultural land at low prices and then to convert it into urban property or a factory zone, reaping enormous profits. In this circumstance, the villagers, since they are collectively landowners with a common vested interest in the land, have often been able to resist land requisitions through mass protests. This has, in fact, comprised the single most frequent type of mass protest in China. Farmers would be more vulnerable and less able to mount such protests – which sometimes are successful – if they were atomised private smallholders, with some families dispossessed of their land and others not.

For all these reasons, it is welcome news that the Third Plenum has given the national leadership's firm public support to the retention of collective landholdings. The Plenum has also gone further, by announcing that 'we will vigorously promote farmers' stockholding cooperatives (*gufen hezuo* 股份合作)' (Article 21). Again, let me explain.

While in some parts of China that are urbanising, local governments requisition the land and residences of villager small groups and the farmers are left with inadequate compensation,[6] in some other regions the villager small groups get to keep much of their land during industrialisation or urbanisation – and their members sometimes benefit greatly in the process. This is often, in fact, usually the case in the Pearl River Delta region of Guangdong province in southern China, and it can also be found in other regions in China.[7] In these places, the rural land collectives also normally transform themselves into shareholding property cooperatives or shareholding companies, ltd. (*gufen youxian gongzi* 股份有限公司).[8] By doing so, their land becomes less vulnerable to a take-over by higher-level authorities. But these so-called companies are really successors of the village land collectives in disguise. Similar to the past, each small-group member owns a share. Each receives dividends each year from the collective property, and after the land has become urban or industrial property, their dividends sometimes amount to more than the annual incomes of middle-class urban households.

This is what has occurred in most of Guangdong's Pearl River Delta, one of the core areas of industrial globalisation and the source of much of the merchandise that fill our shops. There, because the land remains collective property, villages often remain in place as residential communities, while factories and worker dormitories get built on the surrounding agricultural land in industrial parks owned by the shareholding collectives in their guise as companies. The goods imported from China

---

6   E.g., Sally Sargeson, 'Villains, Victims and Aspiring Proprietors: Framing "Land-losing Villagers" in China's Strategies of Accumulation', *Journal of Contemporary China*, vol. 21/77 (September 2012), pp. 757–77.

7   For instance, Beibei Tang of the Australian National University (ANU) has discovered this to be the case in urbanising villages in the major city of Wuhan in central China and also in the city of Shenyang in Manchuria. Sally Sargeson, also at ANU, has had similar findings for the villages she has studied in coastal Zhejiang province in the Yangtze region.

8   Four case studies of rural land collectives that converted themselves into shareholding companies are discussed in Him Chong and Jonathan Unger, 'The Guangdong Model of Urbanisation: Collective Village Land and the Making of a New Middle Class', *China Perspectives*, No. 2013/3 (September 2013), pp. 33–42. This is also described in Anita Chan, Richard Madsen and Jonathan Unger, *Chen Village: Revolution to Globalization* (Berkeley: University of California Press, 2009), Chapter 13.

by New Zealand businesspeople quite often are manufactured in the industrial parks owned by these rural land collectives.

The Third Plenum appears to encourage the spread of this shareholding system to other parts of China (Article 21), and envisions elsewhere in the Plenum's Decision that during urbanisation and industrialisation it will be important to 'ensure farmers share equally the gains from the added value of land' (Article 22).

But the Third Plenum falls short by not creating a legal framework that supports this. What has enabled villagers in Guangdong and the other areas to retain their collective land during urbanisation and industrialisation is that their local governments have been supportive. But in many other parts of China, local governments depend heavily upon the revenues generated by requisitioning rural land inexpensively and then converting the property very profitably into factory sites and urban neighbourhoods. It has been estimated that in China as a whole, in 2010 almost three quarters of local government revenues derived from this source.[9] At the same time, the national leadership is worried about this requisitioning of land, since it is the single greatest cause of social unrest in China. Since local governments will not willingly give up this source of revenue, the Third Plenum needed to find a means to enable villages to benefit directly by converting their land directly to urban or industrial use, bypassing the local governments' land confiscations.

While rhetoric is contained in the Plenum's declarations that favours enabling the villagers to benefit in this way, does the national leadership actually plan to achieve this? The answer, in brief, is that the Third Plenum chickened out. Again let me explain. A hurdle to the conversion of rural collective land into urban land is that, under current law, all urban land must first be categorised as state land, a system in which very long-term user rights are then provided to the owners of urban buildings. When cities expand, only governments at county level and above are authorised to convert the rural collective land into urban state land. County and city governments can take advantage of this situation, and during the process of converting the rural land's status into state land they often take over the land with low compensation. The Plenum Decision indicates that the national leadership recognises the benefits of eliminating this land-conversion requirement.

But China's leadership ultimately has provided only a sop to the villages. Government regulations divide rural land into four types: agricultural land, village residential land, useless waste land, and 'rural construction land' (*jianshe yong di*). The Plenum declared that henceforth only rural construction land 'should be allowed to be directly sold or leased on the market with the same rights and at the same prices as state-owned land' (in Article 11). What is 'rural construction land'? It is land that has been in use as a village factory or a primary school site or some similar public

---

9 Samson Yuen, 'China's New Rural Land Reform? Assessment and Prospects', *China Perspectives*, no. 1 (2014), p. 63.

function. This is estimated to account for only about 4 per cent of village land.[10] The Plenum excluded agricultural land from being released directly on the market without first undergoing a conversion into state land. Since farmland comprises the bulk of rural land, it leaves villages near cities at the mercy of the authorities. When all is said and done, it appears that the national government does not want the financial burden of having to subsidise China's rural governments and is leaving their main source of revenue in place.

Similarly, the Plenum decided cautiously that the villages' residential land should only be allowed to be sold on the market in selected trial 'pilot areas' (Article 21). Outside of such experimental pilot districts, villagers who live within striking distance of cities will continue, for the time being, to be blocked from profitably putting their house sites up for sale on the urban market. The need to have government authorities approve its conversion into 'state land' remains intact. The Plenum took a step in the right direction when it decided to allow the so-called rural construction land to enter the market without conversion into state land, but it was a baby step. When it came to the brink the Party backed off from taking more meaningful steps.

To sum up, what is significant is the Third Plenum's unanticipated re-endorsement of China's system of rural collective property, and the Plenum's endorsement of retaining collective property during urbanisation by way of converting the collectives into shareholding property companies owned by the villagers. But it will take another, future Plenum to muster the courage to prevent local governments from confiscating the rural collectives' land whenever doing so suits the local governments' purposes.

---

10 Ibid., p. 64.

A peaceful and compliant urban labour force is integral to the success of China's reform program; but even as workers' real wages rise and the Chinese economy starts to become less dependent on labour-intensive manufacturing, worker unrest remains a problem, and one that factory managers and owners as well as local officials often seem unable to cope with. The Third Plenum was a good opportunity for the central authorities to put in place new solutions. But Professor Anita Chan argues here that the Plenum's policy proposals in this field turned out to be inadequate.

The Chinese Trade Union Federation at the Crossroads – Relaxing Control over Labour or Risking Labour Instability

Anita Chan

As the number of mass incidents (群众事件) has continued to rise in the past decade, the paramount concern of the Chinese Communist Party (CCP) has become one of maintaining social stability. One of the major types of 'mass incident' has been labour protests. For some years the CCP has delegated to the All-China Federation of Trade Unions (ACFTU) a responsibility to contain labour unrest before it explodes into bigger and more organised and violent disturbances. How the ACFTU handles this mission impossible is the subject of this presentation. The ACFTU needs to devise a balancing act between relaxing pressures and not letting things get out of hand. Does the CCP's Third Plenum Decision of November 2013 have anything to contribute to helping with this balancing act?

I will first identify some fundamental issues faced by the ACFTU. Then I will discuss whether the several labour-related Articles in the Third Plenum's Decision are likely to have any impacts on the union federation and labour.

China's neglect of core labour rights
As labour unrest increased in the late 1990s the CCP began pressuring the ACFTU to find solutions. However, being under the constraint of the Chinese Trade Union Constitution, the ACFTU cannot deviate from the 'guidance of the Party', meaning that both union and workers have little room to act independently.

In the mid-2000s the ACFTU came up with a new policy that, if successful and rolled out in China, would have changed the industrial relations landscape. It would have let workers elect their own trade union branches at workplaces without the

ACFTU losing control, and then move on to what the Chinese union titles 'collective consultations' (集体协商) with management. For the ACFTU, this would have killed two birds with one stone. China would have partially adopted the terms of the two core labour rights Conventions of the ILO (International Labour Organization): Convention no. 87, Freedom of Association and Protection of the Right to Organise, and Convention no. 98, The Right to Collective Bargaining (neither of which it has ratified). From the point of view of ACFTU's own institutional self-interest, first, it might finally have been welcomed into the fold of international trade unions. This is a status that the ACFTU had aspired to for some years. Second, it would have stabilised industrial relations. Labour history shows internationally that organised labour representation has helped stabilise industrial relations.

Thus in 2006, when the Communist Party renewed its pressure on the ACFTU, the union federation initiated a new thrust by secretly organising employees at eighteen Walmart stores to elect their own workplace union committees without Walmart's knowledge (as opposed to being appointed by upper level trade union officials together with management). The elections were genuinely democratic. This marked the ACFTU's first ever attempt to take a small step towards honouring ILO Convention no. 87. Unfortunately, within a matter of weeks the ACFTU reversed this new initiative. It came to an agreement with Walmart that management and trade unions would together decide on who to appoint to be 'elected' to trade union branch committees. With this, the democratic elections came to an end. After that the ACFTU launched a nationwide campaign to have so-called 'direct elections' (直选), which meant pro forma elections directly controlled by local trade unions and/or management. The use of the word 'direct' is to avoid using the word 'democratic'.

One of the paramount functions of any trade union is to carry out collective bargaining with management. Interestingly, China has always recognised what it calls 'collective consultation', which approximates 'collective bargaining', but with Chinese characteristics. There is a fundamental difference between the two. Collective consultation assumes a non-adversarial relationship between management and labour and assumes the consultative outcome is a win-win situation for both parties, while collective bargaining is premised on an adversarial relationship between the two parties and assumes a zero-sum negotiated outcome. 'Collective consultation' is a turn of phrase used to avoid recognising class conflict between capital and labour. Yet gradually 'collective bargaining' has been slipping into the official vocabulary, since after all the reality is any labour dispute is born out of an adversarial relationship between management and labour. The ACFTU has been accepting, indeed requesting, collective-bargaining training programs from foreign trade unions, indicating it implicitly recognises the adversarial relationship.

A question is: why is the Chinese government willing to accept collective bargaining but not freedom of association, even though freedom of association whereby workers can have their own elected union representation is normally a precondition for collective bargaining? Without genuine representation it is not possible to have genuine collective bargaining. The Communist Party and the ACFTU have no intention of letting workers have their own representation. They are side-stepping the crux of the matter and are determined to maintain their tight control over labour. At the grassroots level in China, labour advocates, labour scholars, and even trade union officials have been discussing and debating these issues in conferences for some years. The Party and the ACFTU are caught in a contradictory situation, as any liberalisation of grassroots union organisation is a double-edged sword.

The Third Plenum Decision – a document of little significance for labour

The Third Plenum Decision basically reiterates the status quo in the Party's stance toward labour and the ACFTU. The Decision's various vague policy statements on labour will not take China's industrial relations system in a new direction. The Party is caught in a dilemma of how to attain labour harmony, one of the most important priorities of the ruling authorities.

Let us go through the relevant Articles of the Plenum Decision. Article 44 refers to improving the wage collective consultative negotiation system, but only in passing, without specifying any substantive new suggestions. Notably, it still uses the phrase 'collective consultation' rather than 'collective bargaining'. It does not address the fact that even though the phrase 'collective consultation' was inserted into the Chinese Labour Law more than twenty years ago and the ACFTU has launched campaign after campaign to set up these consultative meetings, almost nothing has changed.

Another example: Article 29 of the Decision proclaims a desire to improve 'democratic management' (民主管理) in enterprise institutions and in public institutions (企业单位, 事业单位), and specifically mentions the 'staff and workers representative congress' (职工代表大会) as the basic democratic management system of these institutions. This oft-used Party expression 'democratic management' has been on the books for many years. To hail the staff and workers congress as a basic democratic system is not new either. When Deng Xiaoping began launching enterprise reforms in the early 1980s, he re-established the staff and workers representative congresses in state-owned enterprises as a means to offset slightly the increased authority that was being granted to company management. A few years later, in 1987–88, the ACFTU even argued that an article should be inserted into the Labour Law that the congress was to be the highest authoritative institution in an enterprise. Reformists in the ACFTU were then aggressively promoting the staff and workers congress as a potential defender of labour in China's transition to capitalism. In doing so the ACFTU had to contend with pro-capital and pro-management bureaucratic interests. But in the 1990s, as enterprise reforms steamed ahead, resulting in the lay-off of millions of state enterprise workers, the role of the congress was smothered. Since then in most state enterprises it has become either a defunct or a formalistic institution, only to be dragged out to legitimise management decisions. In a few rare cases workers have 'discovered' the congress's authoritative power that is written in law and have used it to confront management. But this is so rare that the rhetoric in the Decision about staff and worker congresses reads like platitudes and rings hollow to the ear.

Of note is that the Decision does not touch on the issue of democratic elections of trade union committees. This is indicative of the Party's reluctance to let the ACFTU renew anything akin to the earlier Walmart union election programme of 2006. In sum, the Decision has not outlined any breakthrough that can move China closer to recognising the two ILO core labour rights conventions that some reformists in the ACFTU would like to see.

However, the Decision does reiterate a number of Party/government efforts to 'improve', 'deepen' and 'advance' existing policies, which if implemented will help workers' livelihoods. For instance, Articles 43, 44 and 45 of the Decision promise to create higher employment, do away with discrimination in hiring practices, improve the setting of the minimum wage, provide a fairer distribution of income in society and a fairer social security system, narrow the gap between urban and rural disparities, and so forth. These are not new proclamations. Could the Decision have proclaimed otherwise? The minimum wage, for instance, has been increasing at a double-digit rate annually in the past seven years. This has been beneficial to migrant factory workers, whose wage levels tend to hover close to the minimum wage. To workers, the main issues are unpaid or underpaid overtime work, wage cheating and excessive overtime, issues that have remained fairly unchanged in the past two decades. Based on my detailed computation of wage data collected in my research projects, when the monthly wage is converted into an hourly wage, the actual wage level is generally lower than the legal wage by about 30 per cent due to underpayments in the large amount of overtime work. This problem has been near-universal in the foreign-funded industrial sector for many years, though it also exists in the state sector. The root cause is lack of enforcement by local authorities and the ACFTU.

The Decision's significant impact lies in what it has avoided confronting. It says nothing about labour unrest; it tenaciously sticks to the expression 'collective consultation'; and it is silent on the emergence of some 60 million dispatch (temp agency) workers in the labour market in both the manufacturing and service industries. Nor is there any reference to workers' participatory role. All in all, as far as labour is concerned the Decision is just a goodwill gesture, projecting China as a nation of well-being and social harmony aspiring to attain Xi Jinping's 'China Dream'.

The ACFTU's reaction to the Third Plenum Decision
How has the ACFTU responded to the Third Plenum Decision? The day after the closing of the Third Plenum, the front-page article in *Workers Daily* reaffirmed that the ACFTU is a mass organisation under Party leadership, that it would be of service

to the Party and the state, working towards the common good, and that it would raise high the banner of socialism with Chinese characteristics. The language was trite and full of Maoist-era jargon. Two or three weeks later the ACFTU's official website and *Workers Daily* issued a spate of documents, speeches and conference reports eulogising the wisdom of the Decision in deepening reforms. The ACFTU declared that it would propagate the Party's message far and wide to the lower levels of the union, and that union officials would study the Decision with diligence. All this is standard Chinese-style bureaucratic protocol after the announcement of any broad-ranging Party decision.

A fine example of the ACFTU's trite and empty reaction to the Plenum Decision was a 6th December *People's Daily* article penned by Li Jianguo, a Member of the Communist Party Politburo and the ACFTU Chairman. After five lines of praise for the Decision's new ideas and important theory, Li plunged into recounting two special talks Xi Jinping gave to ACFTU officials earlier, in April and October 2013. In one short article he referred to the 'China Dream' eighteen times. Was this just regular bureaucratese, or was Li being especially eager to show off his personal obsequious deference to Xi Jinping? It is difficult to tell, but what comes through very clearly is that the ACFTU would remain subserviently under the Party's absolute control. Li seemed incapable of extracting from the Plenum Decision anything of substance to highlight. His article openly illustrates the big psychological, social and emotional distance between the top Party leadership and lower level trade union units and workers, a gap that at one time Mao had attempted to bridge.

Reality on the ground
The ACFTU is the bureaucracy that has daily interaction with workers. City-level, district-level, and street-level (街道) union officials and staff are at the front line, dealing with labour issues and the increasing incidence of industrial conflicts. They are thrust into a position torn by conflicting demands. By its constitution, the ACFTU's task is to protect workers' legal rights, but at the same time it is also to serve as a transmission belt between workers and the state. In practice, the trade union chairperson at each level is appointed by the party-state at the same level, and not by the trade union one level above. He or she is accountable to the local party-state and not to the workers. Therefore it is quite normal that new union appointees have never previously been involved in trade union work, and might even have been state enterprise managers or officials from some other local bureaucracy whose previous responsibilities had sometimes stood in opposition to the well-being of workers. An official previously in charge of attracting corporations to invest within the district being assigned next to work for the trade union is a good example.

Trade unions therefore have difficulty cultivating a corpus of expertise to resolve industrial relations issues or develop a culture of sympathy for workers' grievances.

Inasmuch as local and regional leaders' promotion criteria are based on success in promoting economic development and social stability, they tend to favour capital and management and the suppression of social unrest. In the rare circumstances where the local party-state is more sympathetic to the plight of workers, the union may have more room to manoeuvre in representing workers' interests. For instance, when Wang Yang was Party Secretary of Guangdong province (2007–13), both the provincial and Guangzhou trade union chairs developed a more sympathetic attitude towards workers. They tried to educate themselves in union matters though engagement with foreign trade unions, invited foreign trade unions and academics to train lower-level union cadres in collective bargaining, and were even openly critical of police suppression of labour protests. But when they retired two years ago, the orientations of these unions changed.

Professor Anita Chan talking about labour rights, with (from left) Professors Anne-Marie Brady, Kerry Brown and Jonathan Unger looking on

Overall, the ACFTU is saddled with inertia despite years of internal discussion about reforming itself. Nonetheless, the labour sphere in China has undergone rapid change. In the second half of the 1990s, the ACFTU had had the herculean task of placating state enterprise workers who were being laid off and of settling severance packages. As the upheaval in the state sector decreased and more state enterprises began to turn in a profit, labour protests in the state sector subsided. The workers' conditions and wages in this sector are relatively good compared to the foreign-funded and private sectors, and management is more apt to comply with the labour laws. Workplace-level union branches in the state sector play the role of management's social-service arm.

The ACFTU's main daily challenge lies in the non-state sector, especially the Asian-owned foreign factory sector which has hired a vast number of migrant workers during the past thirty years. In the 1980s and the first half of the 1990s, when China was less developed, migrant factory workers were fewer in number and less aware of their legal rights and labour disturbances were less frequent. The migrant workers were seen as necessary victims of a new stage of capital accumulation. But in the last twenty years, through the efforts of Hong Kong labour NGOs (non-governmental organisations), and later China's home-grown labour NGOs, propagating workers' legal rights among migrant workers has begun to pay off. Resistance has begun to emerge among these millions of migrant workers. Admittedly their demands are still mostly defensive, protesting against legal violations by employers, but the protests are no longer limited to unpaid wages or illegally long work hours. Workers are beginning to demand that employers make legally mandated but long-ignored contributions to workers' social security pension accounts. Since the ACFTU's Walmart organisation campaign legitimising workers' elections of branch union committees, some workers have been making demands to set up and elect their own workplace union branches.

Here is a brief chronology of cases of workers' protests (which in the past decade or so have expanded in range, as have efforts by local governments to suppress them):

2006 – workers at a small Danish company's factory in China successfully went on strike to demand their own union representation. This was the first trade union branch set up by workers after a strike.

2010 – workers at a Honda parts manufacturing plant demanded an unprecedented 30 per cent pay rise, the removal of their appointed union chair and the election of a new trade union committee.

2011 – five Pepsi Cola bottling plants located in five cities coordinated a protest action to protect their rights against Pepsi's amalgamation with a Chinese company. This was the first attempt at a well-coordinated cross-workplace organisation.

2013 – workers at a company named Deweixin protested over their severance package. One worker was jailed for 300 days, the first case of a worker being criminalised for going on strike.

2013 – workers at a factory of the Ohms corporation fought to elect their own trade union chair, and one year later wanted to recall him and elect another one. This was the first time workers held accountable a union chair that they themselves had elected.

April 2014 – twelve private security guards at the Guangzhou University of Chinese Medicine Hospital went on a peaceful strike over pay and conditions and were convicted for disturbing the peace. Nine of them were sentenced to prison for seven to nine months, the first time such a large group of strikers were sentenced for going on strike.

April 2014 – 48,000 workers at a huge Taiwanese-owned shoe factory went on strike to protest at being cheated by underpayments to their social security accounts. This is the largest strike in the foreign-funded sector since economic reforms commenced in the early 1980s.

What do all these labour protests tell us? Workers' awareness has been rising, progressing from isolated strikes to cross-workplace strikes; from spontaneous incidents to increasingly organised incidents; from small-scale protests to large-scale protests; from protests against legal violations and non-payments of wages, to demands for material improvements and higher wages and a right to organise (but not yet as an autonomous trade union).

How does the ACFTU handle this escalating labour resistance? Its responses have been fraught with internal contradictions. While continuing to call for a more effective collective consultation process in the hope of pre-empting disputes and settling workers' grievances peacefully, it has normally continued to side with management and pro-capital local governments. Instead of helping workers organise their own elected trade union branches, local union officials have often tried to thwart democratic elections every step of the way. While proclaiming they are working towards a harmonious society, they and local government officials have invited the use of physical violence by calling in the police while simultaneously criminalising strike actions.

As the older generation of migrant workers mature and gain more experience, the authorities are increasingly confronted by a migrant labour force that is beginning to demand respect, material gains, and labour rights. The ACFTU has been tasked by the party-state to handle labour dissatisfaction, but the union federation normally remains unwilling to side with labour. Nor will the ACFTU let go of its official monopoly on labour representation.

The ACFTU is caught in a bind of multiple contradictions. The Third Plenum Decision is too vague, too unheeding, and too removed from reality to provide the ACFTU with any solutions to its conundrum.

One element in China's current reform program is evidently to encourage a shift from investment-led growth of the kind that has fuelled China's rapid economic growth to date to a more consumer-oriented economy. One factor affecting the speed of growth in consumer spending is the continuing propensity of many Chinese to save rather than spend, partly so as to cover costs not met by current pension, welfare and health provisions. In addition to pledging to provide for stronger, fairer and more pervasive health and pension schemes nationwide, the Third Plenum addressed this issue by allowing for greater social welfare provision by NGOs (non-governmental organisations), often called social organisations in China. Dr Stephen Noakes assesses this move.

Civil Society and Social Welfare after the Third Plenum

Stephen Noakes

My remarks today are motivated by three questions regarding civil society and social welfare in China. First of all, how and how much does the Decision of the November 2013 Third Plenum affect the role of NGOs in Chinese governance, particularly in the area of social service delivery? Second, what policy changes, if any, can we expect to see as a result of the Plenum Decision? Third, what are the consequences of China's approach to social organisations for the rest of the world, particularly countries like New Zealand, which work closely with China on a variety of development projects, many of which involve local and international non-state partners?

The latest round of changes to the way Chinese social organisations are governed that arise from the Third Plenum Decision is best understood in the broader context of China's evolving non-state sector, particularly during the reform era from 1978 onward. The Third Plenum Decision and coincidental policy changes in the field of NGO management offer insight into what the continued evolution of the non-state sector will look like under President Xi Jinping. In my view, the Plenum Decision aims to build on and extend the role of civil society groups in social welfare provision that began under Xi's predecessors. This has a variety of domestic and international ramifications.

The political context
The growth of social organisations in China began in the early 1990s with the privatisation of many of China's state-owned enterprises. Social organisations, supervised by the state but funded by others, emerged as a means to ease the

financial and practical burden of service delivery formerly borne by state bodies. (There are obviously some exceptions – the World Wildlife Fund was active in China from the time the country's doors opened in the late 1970s, and forged a special working relationship with the Deng Xiaoping leadership, eventually taking the panda as its official logo.) By and large, however, the growing role of NGOs in Chinese governance is a post-Tiananmen trend, connected intimately with the larger process of state-led reform and opening up, and the Party's efforts to shore up public consent for its continued rule. Consequently, domestic and international NGOs now partner with officials and agencies of the Chinese government in a wide array of development areas, including environmental protection, public health, education and infrastructure, among others. Indeed, the state has in many ways come to depend upon the services that NGOs provide. For this reason, some analysts refer to the state-NGO relationship as 'co-dependent' rather than dominated entirely by the state.

The main tension underpinning this relationship, however, is that social organisations in China have no option but to exist in an institutional and legal climate that was not built to accommodate them. Part of the challenge involves a lack of understanding among both the Chinese public and the Chinese government about the role of social organisations in promoting more transparent and accountable government. Many are confronted with burdensome registration requirements, mistrust and occasional harassment by the authorities. Despite more than two decades of experience with social organisations, China retains many of its quintessentially Leninist attitudes and policies toward NGOs.

Nevertheless, recent generations of state leadership recognise the potential value of social organisations and the part they have to play in preserving the rule of the CCP (Chinese Communist Party). As far as the Third Plenum Decision is concerned, the chief aim of the Xi administration is to take a selective approach to the encouragement of NGOs, ensuring that China engages those organisations willing and able to be a source of support for the state by helping it to govern better, more efficiently and more responsibly.

The Third Plenum Decision and China's social organisations
The Decision of the Plenum makes several references to this role of social organisations in governing China. Collectively these suggest an expanded role for NGOs in China's reforms and in its political system as a result of the Plenum Decision.

The first part of the Decision makes a few oblique references to building 'a socialist country with the rule of law, and develop the people's democracy with wider, more adequate and sound participation.' A few paragraphs later, it states that China should ' . . . promote system innovation in the social sector, promote equal access to basic public services, and step up efforts to form a scientific and effective social management system . . . ' Understood in the larger context of the development of Chinese civil society, NGOs and civic groups are a major mechanism by which these goals are accomplished.

This point is made more explicit in later Articles of the Decision. For example, Article 28 explicitly cites social organisation when it refers to 'build[ing] a consultative democracy featuring appropriate procedures and complete segments to expand the consultation channels of the organs of state power, committees of the Chinese People's Political Consultative Conference, political parties, and community-level and social organizations.' Article 29 spells out how civil society is important in local governance, in particular where it states that 'We [the CCP] will improve the democratic management system in enterprises and public institutions with workers and employees' congress as its basic form, [and] strengthen the building of the democratic mechanism in social organisations.'

Articles 42–46 point to the dual role of social organisation in public consultation and participation, and the delivery of social services. Article 42 states: 'We will strengthen the state's function in supervising education, and entrust social organizations to carry out evaluation and monitoring of education.' Here the suggestion is made that civil society groups are an important source of information to the state about how to govern. Article 44 clearly specifies intentions to give civil society groups the tools they need to combat poverty: 'We will improve the tax reduction and exemption system for charitable donations, so as to give full play to the positive role of charity organizations in helping the poor and needy.' Article 46 suggests the same for the field of health care: 'We will encourage private funds to flow to medical services, first supporting them to flow to not-for-profit medical institutions.'

The intentions of the party-state become even clearer in Section 13 of the Plenum Decision (Articles 47–50), entitled 'Making Innovation in the Social Governance System', which carves out a role for civil society groups while taking care to underline the importance of maintaining social order. Article 48 is devoted to '[k]indling the vigour of social organizations':

> We will correctly handle the relationship between the government and society, intensify efforts to separate government administration and social organizations, encourage the social organizations to clarify their rights and obligations, and enforce self-management and play their role in accordance with the law. Social organizations should be commissioned to provide public services that they are apt to supply and tackle matters that they are able to tackle. We will support and develop volunteer service organizations. We will achieve a true disconnection of trade associations and chambers of commerce from administrative departments, prioritize fostering and development of such social organizations as trade associations and chambers of commerce, scientific and technological associations, charity and philanthropic organizations, and urban and rural community service organizations. These organizations can directly apply for registration in accordance with the law when they are established. We will strengthen the management of social organizations and foreign NGOs in China, and guide them to carry out their activities in accordance with the law.

Civil Society and Social Welfare after the Third Plenum

Dr Stephen Noakes talking about civil society and social welfare

Recent policy developments

As the above passage suggests, there is a push for social organisations to play a role in governance, but not all groups in all areas all of the time. The aim of the most recent policy innovations is to encourage the right sorts of civil society organisations to flourish, and to attract support from the right foreign partners. This suggests a continuing suspicion and antipathy towards groups active in the fields of human rights or democratisation, and the intent of the Party to deploy third sector governance capability in ways that are state-serving or reinforcing, or with groups that are at least willing to keep their more incendiary views to themselves. While the state wants and even needs the social services that social organisations provide, they do not want the advocacy. This is the model of civil society the Plenum announcements are designed to address.

This notion is borne out by a series of preliminary policy shifts, beginning in late 2013 and continuing through the first half of 2014. First, oversight of the registration process for social organisations, particularly foreign NGOs, passed from the Ministry of Civil Affairs to provincial Civil Affairs Bureaus, meaning that these groups no longer needed to make contact with national-level authorities as before. Second, infrastructural support has been increased for the creation of new local organisations in China and to allow them to form new partnerships with foreign and international NGOs. This provision includes special tax status for foreign organisations. Perhaps most significantly, international and domestic NGOs can now place recruitment advertisements on TV and radio and in various print media, a practice that previously had not been possible. Anecdotally, some Civil Affairs Bureaus have trialled the registration of small local NGOs without a state sponsor as was legally required in the past.

Altogether, this package of new regulations is meant to make the day-to-day operations of NGOs easier in order to facilitate the role for social organisations in delivering social welfare and improved public consultation spelled out in the Plenum Decision. Such policies are designed to further develop the legal space for social organisations, but in a way that enables both foreign and domestic NGOs to serve the state's development agenda better, not to provide independent criticism or oversight of the state or to undermine its stability – something that remains a major preoccupation of Party leadership.

Implications for partner nations
The Plenum Decision and accompanying policy moves carry important lessons for the global community, in particular those countries seeking deeper engagement with China in the field of international development. Most important of all is the need to understand China's approach to the role of social organisations and how this may affect their involvement with international NGOs and the foreign governments who fund them.

For many of these governments, especially the United States, engaging China was fundamentally about promoting reform from the outside in. Unlike isolation, a policy that had been tried and failed with respect to other socialist states like Cuba, engagement and cooperation with China was supposed to be a way to socialise it to the mores and standards of the international community, and ultimately to transform China into a more responsible global player and citizen. As carriers and stewards of those values, NGOs were the primary instruments by which China would be changed. This is a conversation that is continuing to be held, not only in the United States but in other Anglosphere countries as well, and may be especially germane to New Zealand, which is currently partnered with China on a 'world first' joint venture project in the Cook Islands.

Yet there is wisdom in facing honestly the realities of what can be accomplished by partnering with China. Because a relationship with China is now a must and will continue to be so, front-line activists, NGOs, and the policy-makers who support them need to be cognisant of the motives and methods behind the Chinese approach to engaging international NGOs, make a sober, clear-eyed assessment of the risks, and calibrate their expectations accordingly.

PART TWO
ECONOMIC AND FINANCIAL AFFAIRS

Major reform of the restrictive hukou *or household registration system has been a step many economists and others have been pressing the central authorities in Beijing to undertake for some considerable time. Piecemeal reforms of the system have taken place to date, and more are envisaged under the terms of the Third Plenum Decision. Meanwhile the* hukou *system still prevents those living in rural areas from moving into cities and towns and having the same rights as city dwellers, and in many cases from moving into urban areas at all. Some argue that the* hukou *system has lessened the slum-dwelling hardships suffered by poor people in other big cities in Asia and beyond. But many others make the point that the system is not only inhumane but also uneconomical. Professor Cai Fang puts the case here for a more comprehensive reform of the* hukou *system. In his view this would provide China with a much-needed growth dividend by making the Chinese labour force much larger and more flexible.*

Demographic Dividend to Reform Dividend: *Hukou* [Household Registration] Reform and Its Impact on Economic Growth in China

Cai Fang

Central areas of reform not only bring us justice, equity, equality and equal access to public services; they also bring us a reform dividend, that is a pro-growth type of reform. So as an economist I will talk about the reform of the *hukou* 户口 or household registration system from the perspective of the sustainability of Chinese economic growth.

People have high expectations of the 2013 Third Plenum because like the Third Plenum of 1978, the 2013 Plenum laid out a comprehensive reform agenda in almost every aspect of economic, ecological, political, social and cultural affairs and Party construction. *Hukou* reform is regarded as both an economic reform and a social governance reform. But it is very important for us to know that *hukou* reform is a pro-growth type of reform, because without a consensus on this point the implications of this reform will not be significant even after the Central Committee of the Party has determined on it.

So first let us ask the question: is there a trade-off between this reform and economic growth? In other words is there is a reform dividend, particularly now that the demographic dividend has disappeared? The answer to this has very strong implications, particularly for building a consensus on implementing the reform and the approach we choose to implement it. I will talk about this in what follows.

Professor Cai Fang from the Chinese Academy of Social Sciences talking about *hukou* reform while Professor Xiaoming Huang from Victoria University of Wellington looks on

The chair of panel 2, Professor Xiaoming Huang

Let me start by looking at the economic slowdown in China. Previous speakers have mentioned that in future China will not be able to sustain its two-digit economic growth rate. This is true. In this regard I would like to draw your attention to the fact that the Chinese economy has passed through two turning points, turning points that have strong implications for what I am going to talk about.

The first is the so-called Lewis turning point, as defined by the economist Arthur Lewis. This is the point reached when no more labour can be drawn from the agricultural sector without a significant increase in wages. Most developing countries are dual economies with two sectors. One is agriculture with an unlimited supply of labour, that is a surplus labour force. The other is the non-agricultural or modern industrial sector, whose expansion absorbs the outflow of surplus labour from the agricultural sector.

In 2004 China experienced a labour shortage for the first time. In Chinese we call this *min gong huang* 民工荒, a migrant labour shortage. The phenomenon occurred first in coastal areas and then spread throughout the country. Now if you go to any enterprise and ask the manager what the most difficult issue is in their operation, they will tell you they cannot recruit sufficient workers. They aren't referring to skilled workers, but to unskilled workers, ordinary workers. So after 2004 we have seen a continual labour shortage, and also the fast growth of wages for unskilled workers. The wages of migrant workers, for example, have grown since then at a rate of 12 per cent per annum in real terms.

In 2010 we conducted a population census, and we can see from the census data that the working-age population aged between 15 and 59 peaked in that year, while since then the working-age population has declined in absolute terms. Since 2010 we have therefore seen an absolute reduction in the size of the labour force in China. The beginning of the decline in the size of the Chinese labour force is the second turning point. Put the two turning points together and we can see that China passed the Lewis turning period between 2004 and 2010.

Why are these two turning points so important? As has already been mentioned today, in the past thirty years or so China has had fast growth. This 10 per cent annual growth rate of GDP has benefited mainly from the so-called demographic dividend. Figure 1 shows our calculation of the growth rate in the past three decades divided into different components relating to production factors and productivity. You can see, first, that much the largest contribution to GDP growth has come from capital formation. How can capital formation be relevant to a demographic dividend? First, if there is a demographic transition (a transition from high fertility rates to low fertility rates) with a declining dependency ratio (the ratio of those of the population not in the labour force and those in it) of the kind experienced by China in past decades, there is more surplus to be saved, and that guarantees a higher savings rate. Second, if you have an unlimited supply of labour you do not face the phenomenon of diminishing return to capital. So in past decades the demographic

Figure 1: What's Driven China Growth So Far

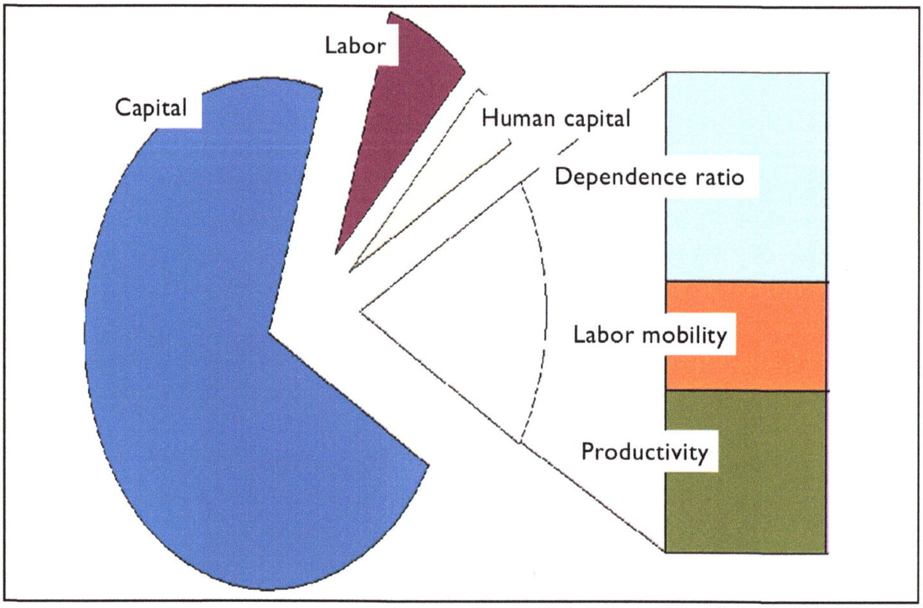

Figure 2: Growth Slows as Dividend Vanishes

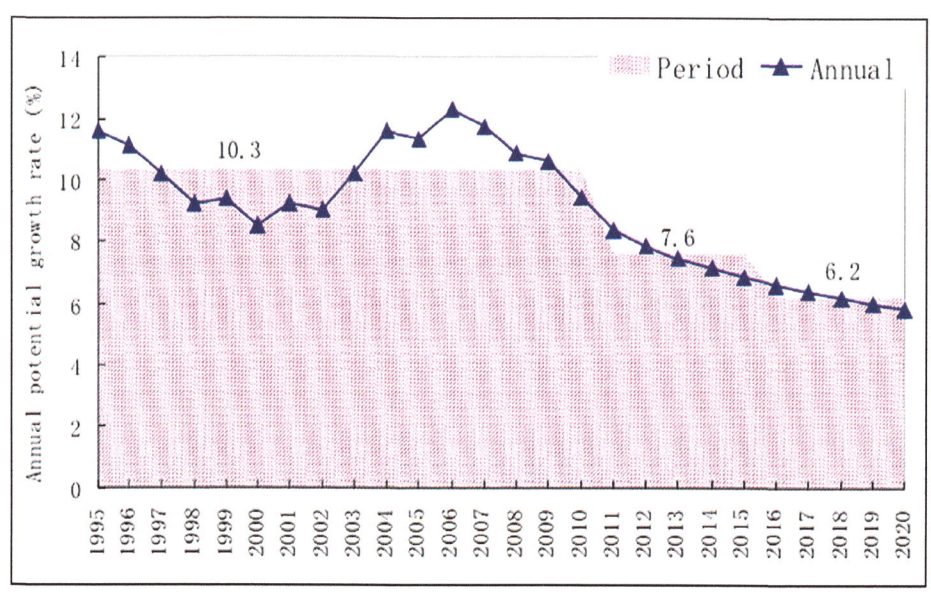

transition guaranteed a high return to capital and a high savings rate.

Other factors, as you can see, are the labour force and human capital (that is, the education of workers), and the dependency ratio (that's a pure demographic dividend). All these contributed to GDP growth. Then there is total-factor productivity growth, and a major part of this productivity growth is attributable to the movement of the labour force from a low productivity sector, agriculture, to a higher productivity sector, the non-agricultural sector. So almost everything achieved in the past came from the demographic dividend.

Since 2010, the working-age population has started to decline, meaning that the demographic dividend is disappearing. So with that we can expect a decline in GDP growth. Figure 2 shows our calculation of the potential growth rate for GDP, the normal GDP growth rate given the supply of production factors and the increase potential of productivity. You can see that in the period 1995 to 2010 the potential GDP growth rate is 10.3 per cent annually. It is declining during the current, Twelfth Five-Year Plan period (2011–2015) to an annual growth rate of 7.6 per cent. Growth in the past two years was actually 7.7 per cent per annum. For the next Five-Year Plan period (2016–2020) it declines further to an annual growth rate of 6.2 per cent. That is mainly because of the disappearance of the demographic dividend.

Therefore a lot of people, for example the famous economist Paul Krugman, have said that China is now in real trouble, and that if it cannot solve many things the Chinese economy will hit a wall, a great wall as we say in Chinese. Therefore we have to know if reform can bring us economic growth, sustainability of growth. In general, when a developing country finishes the cheap labour stage of its economic growth it faces a new era of economic growth; we call this a 'neoclassical scenario.' During this new era it has to rely on innovation, technological progress, total-factor productivity improvement and many other things. But for China there is a special source of further economic growth, namely institutional benefit. I mean that if we eliminate some institutional barriers preventing a sufficient supply of production factors and a significant improvement in productivity we can gain extra economic growth soon. We call this a reform dividend.

There are a lot of areas from which we can benefit to sustain economic growth. A very important one is urbanisation. Early on when Premier Li Keqiang talked about urbanisation he used the term 'a new type of urbanisation'. But most people didn't know what 'new type' meant. In fact on one occasion I told Premier Li that 'maybe you use the word urbanisation with one particular implication, but local governments will think it means a good opportunity to stimulate economic growth by investing more in infrastructure, real estate and many other forms of construction.' Then later on the Premier used a new definition to mean a new type of people-centred urbanisation. So I think it may be appropriate for us to further specify that urbanisation is people-centred, a new urbanisation focusing on transforming migrant workers to legal residents in urban areas. That is *hukou* (household registration) reform.

Every household in China has an ID for the household's registration. The cover of the ID is the same in all cases, but when you open it, the first page shows whether it is an agricultural *hukou* – that is for most farmers who live in the countryside – or another type of *hukou*, a non-agricultural *hukou*. You can also call these two types of *hukou* rural *hukou* and urban *hukou*. With different forms of registration people have different types of access to the public services that social security legally provides. If you remove the barriers, narrowing the gap between the two different types of provision of public services, you have to reform the *hukou* system and integrate the two types of *hukou* into one – making just Chinese citizens. *Hukou* system reform in this way can immediately increase the potential growth rate by stimulating the full supply of labour and more growth of total-factor productivity.

Now, we have in Figure 3 two indicators showing the urbanisation level in China. The official publicised figure is the pink one, showing that currently the urbanisation level is 53 per cent – that is, 53 per cent of Chinese people live in urban areas and have done so for at least six months. This indicator of urbanisation includes migrant workers, because there is another, statistical definition for migrant workers, namely those who have left their township for more than six months. But actually migrant workers do not have an urban *hukou*, and therefore do not have equal access to social security, compulsory education for their children and other public services. So we have another indicator to show the urbanisation level with Chinese characteristics, that is the proportion of the urban population with urban or non-agricultural *hukou*. That is the second, dark blue line, which is 36 per cent at present. The difference between the pink and dark blue lines is migrant workers. If we narrow the gap between the two lines, the two meanings of urbanisation, that is *hukou* system reform.

For migrant workers living and residing in urban areas without local *hukou* there is much poorer provision of social security programmes. For example with the pension system, 60 per cent of those with urban *hukou* are covered by public pensions, while only 13 per cent of migrant workers are. This is because of segregation by *hukou* status, which makes migrants' residence and work unstable. You know, migrant workers are highly mobile, and when they leave one city they usually withdraw what they have contributed, and so lose the continuation of their pension programme. The *hukou* system also prevents agriculture from being modernised. In China we call the agricultural labour force the 386199 force, since 3/8 means March 8, Women's Day, 6/1 means June 1, Children's Day, and 9/9 means September 9, which in the traditional Chinese calendar is Old People's Day. In other words, when all the young people migrate to the urban areas, their parents, children, and sometimes their spouses are left behind in the agricultural areas. So agriculture lacks economy of scale because of small pieces of land that remain less productive than they should be.

Figure 3: Incomplete Urbanisation So Far

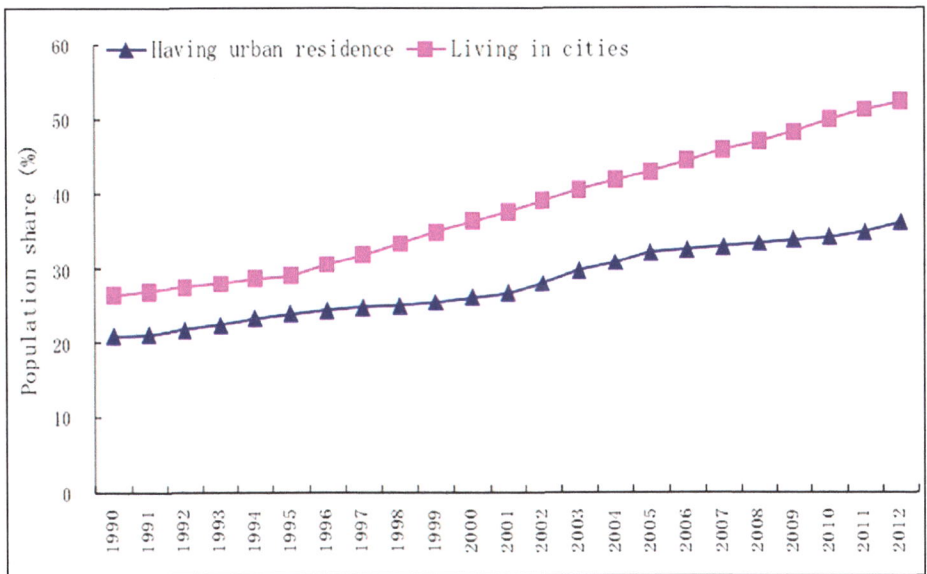

So reform of the *hukou* system can have the effect of killing three birds with one stone. One bird is the labour supply. Give labourers equal access to local social welfare and they can supply a stable labour force and work until they retire. The ANU (Australian National University) labour economist Meng Xin has found that while individual Chinese migrants' wages can increase for more than twenty years in the urban labour market, they live and work in the urban labour market for only nine years on average. That is to say that the *hukou* system prevents them from providing a sufficient supply of labour.

Hukou reform can also reallocate the labour force between different sectors, thus generating improvements in productivity. By increasing farmers' and migrants' incomes, *hukou* reform will also reduce China's Gini coefficient, thus achieving economic rebalancing. We estimate that new-type urbanisation (*hukou* reform) will contribute more than a trillion yuan of GDP each year through an increased labour force participation rate, increased working hours and increased total-factor productivity.

Today people have mentioned low-hanging fruit. When there is low-hanging fruit there are a lot of opportunities to reform. We usually call this kind of reform 'Pareto improvement' (named after the economist Vilfredo Pareto) – that is, it benefits some people without hurting anyone else. But now, after thirty-five years of reform, there are fewer and fewer opportunities for Pareto improvement, and instead we should seek 'Kaldor improvement' reform (named after the economist Nicholas Kaldor) – that is, if you know the reform will bring benefit in general, you can provide compensation to those who are losing from it.

That said, one problem is that in China the cost of *hukou* reform tends to be overestimated. Most city mayors would estimate that we have to pay a lot of money for *hukou* reform because there are a lot of subsidies in public services. So now megacities are excluded from the *hukou* reform agenda. That is a problem. Also some cities only offer migrant workers residence cards instead of *hukou*. That reminds me of the so-called Beijing green card that was issued by the Beijing municipal government to attract foreign experts. For many years, only a few foreigners actually got this green card. (The famous economist Robert Mundell was one.)

What my colleagues and I have deduced is that *hukou* reform really can bring a dividend to general economic growth. So we can take at least a certain part of this dividend to compensate for or share the cost of urbanisation among central and local governments and different regions. Therefore in conclusion I should say that *hukou* reform is a needed measure to help sustain economic growth by increasing China's potential growth rate. So it is a high priority for further reform.

The Third Plenum Decision pledges to 'further rationalise division of revenue through tax reform', and notes that centre-local fiscal relations are on the agenda for reform. The Decision also provides for local governments to be able to issue bonds so as to manage their very substantial debts. These debts have been incurred by under-resourced local governments so as to fund China's impressive local infrastructure development, and have depended in part on opaque shadow-banking arrangements. Despite the Third Plenum's initiatives, local government debt in China remains a concern, and Professor Christine Wong explains here why in her view it is a threat to China's financial and macro-economic stability.

Public Financial Management in China: Fiscal Decentralisation and the Challenge of Containing Local Government Debt

Christine Wong

I agree with David Shambaugh when he says that China is at another turning point, and that there is a real sense of urgency that this is the do-or-die moment; that if certain reforms don't get implemented in the next few years, China will face very serious difficulties. Wen Jiabao in his final speech as Premier, his 'Report on the Work of Government' to the NPC (National People's Congress, or parliament) in March 2013, again used the four 'un-'s, those famous four words he first used in 2007, namely that the Chinese economy is 'unstable, unbalanced, uncoordinated and unsustainable'.

In his Explanatory Note on the Third Plenum Decision, Xi Jinping called reform of the fiscal system one of China's priorities. This is the first time since *fenshuizhi* 分税制, the tax-sharing system reforms introduced in 1994, that inter-governmental reform, centre-local relations, is on the agenda for fiscal reform. And I want to talk today about local government debt, the looming local government debt, and the threat it poses to the financial and macro-economic stability of China, being a very key driver of the urgency not just for fiscal reform but for inter-governmental fiscal reform.

Local government debt has been an issue in China for some time. When I worked in the World Bank office in China in the 1990s, local government debt was already an issue. We were asked to provide technical assistance on how other countries kept track of it. But nothing much was done, and only the Ministry of Finance seemed worried about it. No audits were ever conducted during the period from the beginning of reform in 1979 to 2010. It finally reached a top policy-level agenda towards the end of 2009 and the beginning of 2010, when the CBRC (China Banking Regulatory Commission) noticed that about one third of all credit was being grabbed up by things called 'local government financial platforms'. The CBRC asked, what are these things? how many of them are there? what have they borrowed money to do? They didn't have any information. They went to the central bank, but the central bank didn't have any information either. Then they started to worry. The Ministry of Finance knew what these platforms were but didn't know how many there were. No agency knew. So toward the end of 2010 they finally decided they'd better do a national audit.

Bear with me while I go through some numbers. In 2011, the Chinese National Audit Office conducted the first nationwide audit, with 41,300 auditors who tromped around the country, auditing three levels of government – province, prefecture and county. They visited 25,590 government agencies and audited the books of 6,576 local government financial platforms. They came up with numbers; and immediately there was a national outcry that the numbers were wrong. They had undercounted because they were only addressing themselves to the question: how much is government on the hook for? But that's a narrow question. The broader and more relevant questions to ask are: how much is really being borrowed? what is the borrowing for? and what are these platforms – how do you define a local government financial platform as opposed to just a financial company?

Professor Christine Wong from the University of Melbourne talking about local government debt

In 2012–2013 over a three-month period they did a sample audit of thirty-six local governments – fifteen provinces and their capital cities, three province-level cities and three districts under them – and found that there had been an alarming increase in debt since the 2011 audit, which had looked at the books up to year-end 2010. So they decided they needed another nationwide audit. This was done in 2013 and conducted over a two-month period with 54,400 auditors. This time they decided to audit all five levels of government: central, province, prefecture, county and township. That added up to 62,215 government agencies and 7,170 local government financial platforms.

The source of the worry, as outlined in Figure 4, is this. In 2010 when CBRC first noticed that there was a problem, the government ordered banks to stop lending to local governments and local government financial platforms. The first line in the figure shows the amount of debt to the end of 2010, as identified by the first nationwide audit. At that time local governments at the three levels audited had direct debt of 6.7 trillion yuan, with additional guaranteed debt of 2.3 trillion yuan and then partially guaranteed debt and so on. The next line in the figure shows what was found in the second nationwide audit, to the end of June 2013. Direct debt came out at 10.9 trillion, an increase of 62 per cent. This was after the government had said no more bank lending to local governments and local government financial platforms. And when you add everything together (depending on how you do that, and whether you count only government debt, which is direct debt plus guaranteed debt, or also include contingent or partially guaranteed debt) combined debt came out at 13.6 trillion or 17.9 trillion yuan.

Figure 4: The Source of the Worry

Unit: trn¥ Date	Direct Debt	Guaranteed Debt	Partially Guaranteed	Columns 1+2 only	Combined Debt
End 2010	6.7	2.3	1.7	9.0	10.7
End June 2013	10.9	2.7	4.3	13.6	17.9
Change	4.2	0.3	2.7	4.5	7.2
Increase	62%	14%	150%	50%	57%

What this says is that the central government's efforts to clamp down on local borrowing completely and utterly failed. One point we should note is that the second audit was a much more careful audit that flushed out all the hidden debts of local governments. So it may be that the debt was not all new debt, it just hadn't been properly counted the first time round. But in any case the picture is still that the central government's clampdown efforts failed. And to this day the central

Figure 5: Contagion Effects on the Rest of the Economy

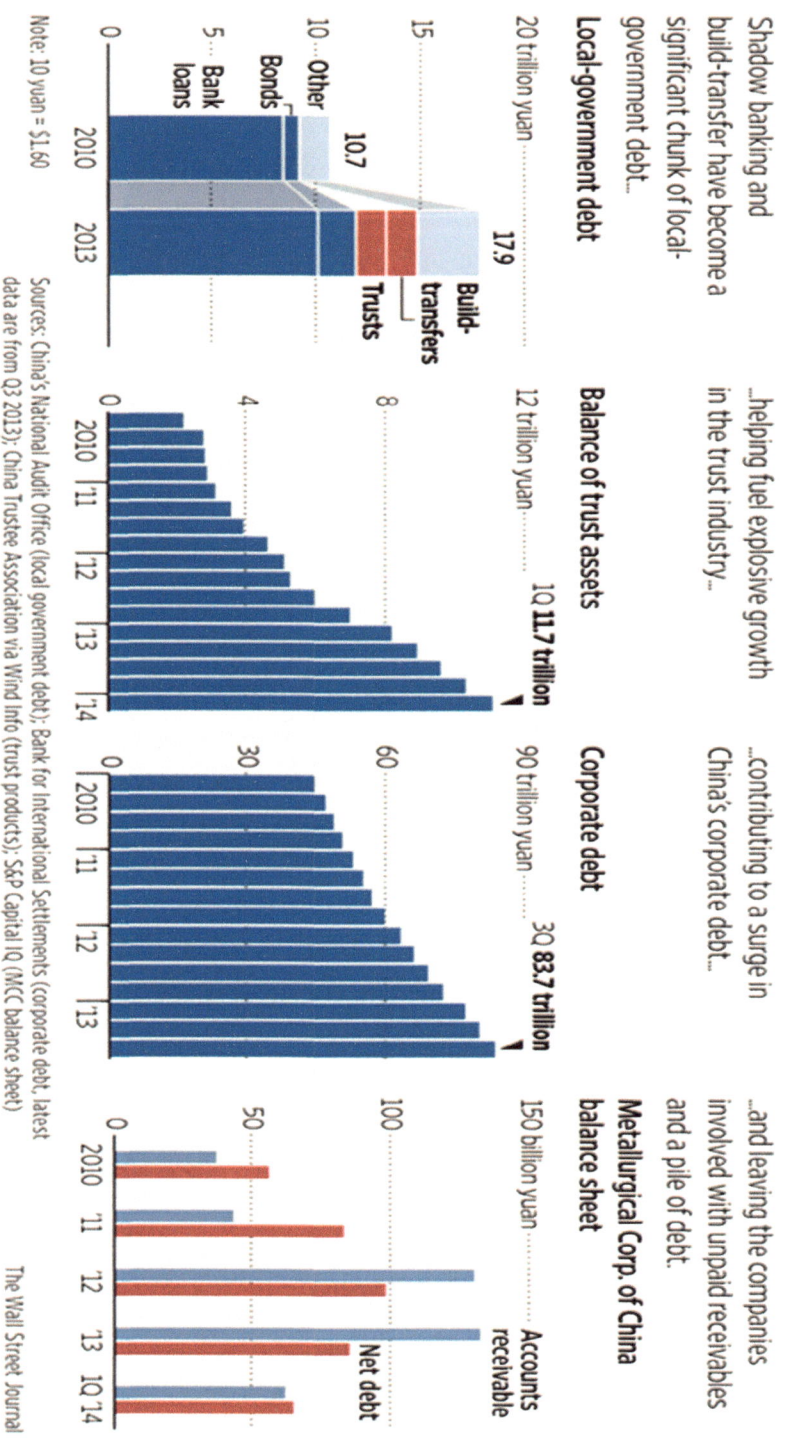

Source: The Wall Street Journal

government doesn't know how much local governments have borrowed. In addition there is the issue of whether the central government knows what the borrowing is for, whether or not it is for the creation of real assets that can generate incomes, allowing GDP to provide a growing tax base, and so on.

Figure 5, from the *Wall Street Journal*, gives a very helpful picture of how this affects the rest of the Chinese economy – the contagion effect that this can have. The first graph in the chart shows debt from 2010 to 2013. The dark blue bars are bank loans and bond issues, so these are explicit debt from the banking sector; they show that growth slowed, although it didn't stop. The government said stop, but it didn't stop. (Actually the government said stop but then afterwards said, in effect, 'Well, go ahead with this and that issue because in many cases if local governments stop borrowing altogether they won't be able to meet payroll. You can't have that going on.' So the banks issued some new loans.)

What the graph also shows is that between 2010 and 2013 non-banking sector debt grew very rapidly. This is shown by the red and light blue parts of the 2013 bar, which represent the shadow banking stuff that everyone talks about. It's very hard to count, and it's very hard to figure out how much damage it could cause. The red bar partly represents trust loans. A trust loan is one that is handled by a bank but isn't bank money – the bank is not legally lending its money to somebody, it's just taking money from one source, usually corporations, SOEs (state-owned enterprises), and acting as an intermediary in issuing a document that says the money is now entrusted through the bank to be lent to somebody else.

So local governments do not now have access to bank loans. They go to the banks, the banks talk to some SOE down the block, which can borrow money from the bank at subsidised interest rates and lend at much higher interest rates to whoever wants to take the resulting trust product. Banks are also taking loans to local government financial platforms that they can't get the money back on. They dress them up, print some papers called wealth management products, and send them out the door. (Americans have a lot of experience with these things.) So we don't really know what's happened; but there is an awful lot of borrowing still going on.

Let me turn now to the issue of why there is so much local government borrowing in China, and why in a country like China with a strong central government the central government doesn't know about it – why the borrowing is a surprise for it. First, there is the systemic issue of fiscal decentralisation. China is very decentralised in terms of local government, delivery of services, local government spending, etc. The problem, which has been around since the beginning of reform, is that there is a very great mismatch between revenue and expenditure at the local level. Local governments only get 50 per cent of national revenue in aggregate, and are asked to deliver 85 per cent of all government spending. Even sociologists can tell you that there is a gap there!

On top of that there is urbanisation. From 1978 to 2010, 500 million people either moved to cities or lived in places that came to be incorporated as parts of cities. So during that period there was a 500 million-plus increase in the urban population. There are lots of benefits to urbanisation – economies of scale, higher productivity and so on – but urbanisation is very expensive. If you have people living in cities, you have to build streets, water pipelines, gas pipelines, power plants, etc. etc. Urbanisation requires infrastructure, enormous amounts of infrastructure. And infrastructure investments have of course taken place in China on a large scale. Anyone who goes to China cannot fail to be impressed by this enormous catch-up. Old people – like me – remember how, walking down the streets of Nanjing in the late 1970s, they would find honey buckets turned upside down on major boulevards in daylight because people were drying them out, because they didn't have sewers then.

China now has world-class infrastructure. This costs money. And infrastructure development has been the responsibility of local governments that haven't had enough money in their budgets. Across the world, governments invest in infrastructure by borrowing. I could give you a whole lesson on why that is both efficient and equitable; but anyway the fact is that you usually need to borrow money to spend on long-term capital. But the budget law in China prohibits local governments from borrowing unless they get explicit permission from the State Council (the cabinet-level central government). So in China you have local governments that have been forced to deal with urbanisation, need infrastructure investment, don't have enough money, and have somehow coped – because it's China.

Figure 6 shows the local government share of total spending and public investment in China. They two have gone in step, so that by 2007, 70–80 per cent of local spending and investment was being done by local governments. The second graph in Figure 6 shows the share of public investment financed by the budget. Since the late 1980s that has been less than 5 per cent. The costs of infrastructure and urbanisation in China have been borne by local governments, mostly at the municipal level, on the basis of land revenues and borrowing; and they borrow through special financial vehicles because they are not allowed to borrow on the government's account.

Management of public investment is by far the weakest part of the fiscal system (and the whole fiscal system in China has many problems). No agency has comprehensive oversight of what government is borrowing and investing in because it's been moved off the budget, it's not within the Ministry of Finance's purview, not part of what it does. It used to be that the State Planning Commission (now the National Development and Reform Commission, or NDRC) and its counterparts at the local level approved all capital investments of the government. But in 2005 the Commission had to give up administrative approval of large projects. From 2005 onwards, the NDRC or its local counterparts no longer needed to approve projects if the projects were not primarily funded by government.

Public Financial Management in China

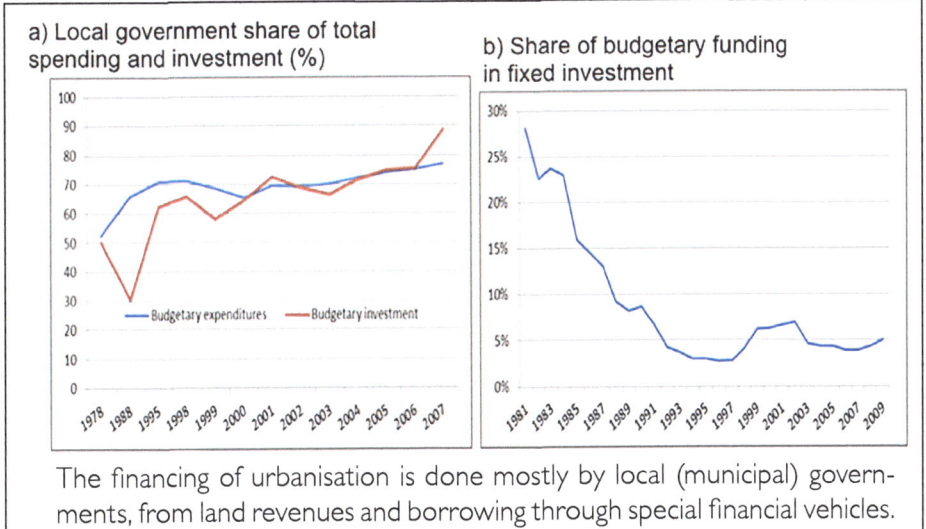

Figure 6: The Financing of Urbanisation

The financing of urbanisation is done mostly by local (municipal) governments, from land revenues and borrowing through special financial vehicles.

Here's the problem: what is the definition of government or public funds? Some provinces – Guangdong, Jiangsu and Zhejiang for example – say in effect, 'Oh we know what that means – it means budgetary funding. So if it's not from the budget, it's not from public funds.' So in their cases nothing requires administrative approval. In some of the poorer provinces things may be different. But we should remember that much of this was happening in the period 2005 to 2010–11, when money was readily available. Chinese GDP was growing at more than 10 per cent a year. The attitude was, you build it and they will come, and so nobody was terribly worried. And no government in China had a balance sheet, not even the central government. The Ministry of Finance has been trying since the 1990s to set up mechanisms for monitoring and controlling borrowing and fiscal risks. But the Ministry doesn't have the authority; nobody pays attention to it. It is just one agency among many.

If I had more time I would talk more about how other countries go about controlling and monitoring local government debt. In most countries local governments are responsible for public investment. Among member states of the OECD (Organisation for Economic Co-operation and Development) they are responsible on average for about 70 per cent of public investment, and the fiscal risk of local government borrowing is very high. Local governments are responsible for delivering social expenditures, welfare, education, health services and so on. They are usually very dependent on transfers. They customarily have very limited taxing power, and public financial management systems are usually weaker at the local government level. Then you have moral hazards (situations in which people take risks because they believe the potential costs will be met by others) – the moral hazards of local governments and their creditors, who may expect that if they really get into trouble a higher level of authority will bail them out.

There are many instances in many countries of local government fiscal problems spilling over. Various mechanisms and institutions have been set up to try and prevent this happening. Some countries, the US being the prime example, rely on the market for discipline. If you buy a local government bond in the US and the local government goes belly up – there have been examples of this in New York City, Orange County California, Detroit – then it's you as the creditor who loses. You bought a bond, and you lose.

But market discipline requires a local government that cannot be guaranteed by higher levels. Creditors are not in any way coerced into providing loans, and full information is provided on local government liabilities. Local governments react rationally, care about default, and do not speculate on bailout. None of these conditions are met in China.

Other countries rely on fiscal rules that limit the amount and uses of local borrowing. These also require institutional support, such as a legal framework, a comprehensible reporting system, an enforcement regime, a penalty and redress regime – conditions that are also missing in China.

Finally, local government incentives remain very much biased toward growth and investment. I was in Henan province at the end of April, and I found that local government incentives there have not changed since the end of the central government's 2008–2009 fiscal stimulus programme or since the 2013 Third Plenum. The first-priority task for local government at all levels – province, municipality, county – is to promote economic growth and national development. If you look at the Henan provincial government's latest Report on the Work of Government, the first five items in the report are all about investment. Every third- or fourth-tier city we visited is planning for huge growth despite the fact that if you look at the population of Henan province between 2005 and 2010, the year of the most recent national population census, the province had a net outflow of 12 million people. Henan is a poor province; people go to big cities and coastal areas to work; and yet senior officials there are still planning for ambitious investments based on borrowing.

Getting local governments in China up to speed on debt management and building a framework for monitoring it is going to take a long time. It's going to take a lot to implement institutional change. But what's the alternative? Can the tasks of investing in infrastructure be centralised so that the central government can do it itself? The answer I think is 'no', because as Figure 7 shows, the administrative structure in China is as decentralised as the fiscal system. Central government is very small. There are only 59,000 people working for the central government. The Ministry of Finance has only a thousand people. The NDRC has another thousand

Public Financial Management in China

– and so on. Yet the central government is very ambitious, it has a lot of money to spend, and it wants to do a great many things. It depends on local governments to deliver and to comply with what it wants to do. And that's a really hard job. It seems that China has outgrown its government/administrative structure, and the difficulty of reining in local government debt is just one symptom of disarticulation in the system.

Figure 7: The road to reform will be long ... but China has no alternative to a decentralised approach

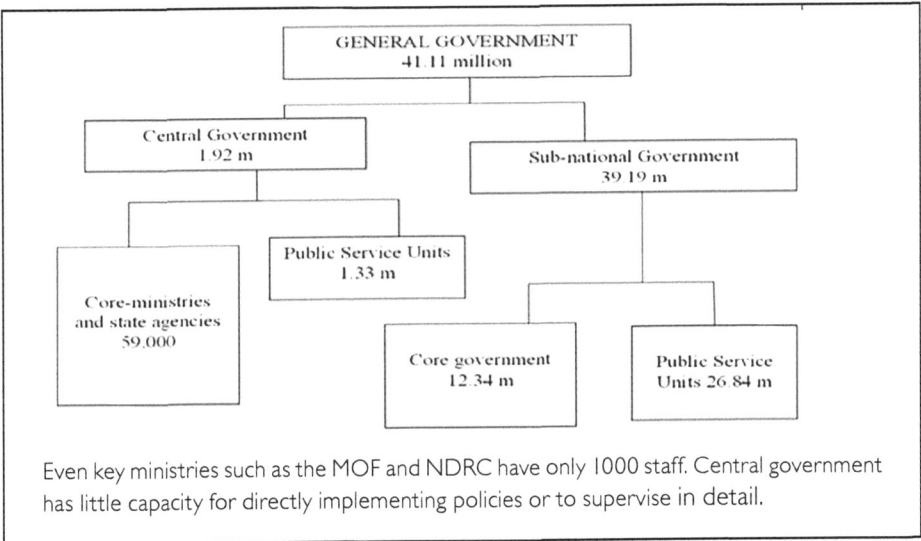

Even key ministries such as the MOF and NDRC have only 1000 staff. Central government has little capacity for directly implementing policies or to supervise in detail.

The Third Plenum has put inter-governmental reform on the agenda, but the intent appears to aim toward centralisation – e.g. more and better transfers rather than more local revenue autonomy. These will likely result in further straining the bureaucracy and producing more distortions.

Some commentators were disappointed that the Third Plenum Decision did little to modify the dominant role of SOEs (state owned enterprises), whilst seeming to propose insufficient measures for the protection of China's increasingly polluted environment. But as Associate Professor Ligang Song argues here, one important provision of the Third Plenum may in fact help make SOEs much more efficient and better tuned to current needs, while also greatly improving environmental protection as well as enhancing consumerism. That is the Third Plenum's move to provide for price reform of water, oil, gas, electricity and services so that their prices are 'determined by the market' in line with the Plenum's decision to give the market the decisive role.

China's Resource Demand, the Environment and Enterprise System Reform

Ligang Song

The first issue I would like to focus on is the relationship between mineral resources, energy and economic growth. When we talk about economic theories, at least in the neo-classical sense, we take capital, labour and TFP (total-factor productivity, a variable that accounts for effects in total output not caused by labour and capital) as the main factors contributing to economic growth. However, people increasingly realise that energy resources are a very important factor too, one that needs to be made explicit in determining economic growth. The China boom in recent decades vividly reflects the role of resources, energy in particular, in determining growth.

So when we talk about China catching up, becoming perhaps the largest economy in PPP (purchasing power parity) terms, when we talk about China as a magnet lifting 300 million people out of absolute poverty as a result of economic reform, when we talk about more than 300 million people entering the middle class as a result of rising per capita incomes, we can see that this is not just the result of capital and labour. Mineral resources and energy also play a very important role. So this is the overarching framework in which we should assess China's growth.

The second issue I want to focus on is why this is a China boom. Over the last decade or so we have seen the speed, scale and intensity of Chinese growth through rapid capital investment, industrialisation, urbanisation, regional development and global integration – all of these elements were behind China's high demand for resources.

The speed of China's growth has been extraordinary – people today have already touched on that – amounting as it does to an average GDP growth rate of about

9.6 per cent per annum over thirty years. The scale of the growth has basically been driven by capital investment. During the past thirty years, average capital investment as a percentage of GDP has totalled about 47 per cent per annum. This is extremely high, compared even with the Asian NIEs (newly industrialised economies) and Japan in their high growth periods. And the intensity of the growth, especially with regard to resources and energy, is again extraordinary. This is the particular angle from which we can look at the impact of China's development on the environment and also at the need for SOE (state-owned enterprise) system reform as part of China's strategy in confronting the challenge of the issue of climate change. I will come back to these issues later on.

Industrialisation in China has come to the middle and increasingly towards the end of the phase in which its production is a very capital-intensive and energy- and resource-intensive. This is easing a bit now as a result of the improvement in China's energy efficiency over the past few years, but high capital-intensive and energy-intensive growth is still the general trend for the time being. Urbanisation has been touched upon and I don't want to repeat what's been said, but just from Christine Wong's data you can see that the urbanisation process is not yet over. And when you talk about natural resources, what mining companies care about most is urbanisation, because urbanisation generates huge demands for infrastructure, residential housing, etc. And these demands translate back into a demand for resources.

Regional development is another dimension to China's boom. China has twenty-eight provinces and six other provincial-level administrative units, and while we can talk about average growth, average figures taking into account all the variables, the fact is that these provinces have vast differences in terms of standards of living, growth and development. The income gap between rich and poor provinces is such that rich provinces can be as much as ten times richer than poor provinces, suggesting that this resource- and energy-intensive phase of industrialisation may be prolonged while those later comers are catching up in their development. So when we talk about the intensity of China's growth, it's not just about growth in China as a whole. We also have to take into account the regional disparities in this growth, which have important implications for China's future demand on resources.

China's boom is partly a story about global integration, as China has relied heavily on exporting, which is a key factor in determining a country's resource intensities, especially metal intensities. The pattern of development of Japan, of Korea and of Taiwan is illustrative. The metal intensities (intensity of demand for different metals) of economic activities in these three places, especially with regard to aluminium and steel, have demonstrated different patterns. The metal intensities of Japan's economic activity rose but then steadily tapered off, whereas Korea is another model. All the metal intensities of Korea rose continuously even after it reached a relatively high level of per capita income. Taiwan is somewhere in between. So the question is whether in this respect China will follow the path of Japan or the path of Korea. That will have tremendous implications for the demand for resources, energy included.

Part of the story of Korea is about global integration because of its very high dependence on exports. As you know, China is in a similar position. China is now the largest manufacturing powerhouse in the world, having surpassed the United States in 2012. It now produces more than 20 per cent of global manufacturing products. A relatively high proportion of these products are for export, and their composition is shifting very rapidly too. In the early phase of reform, China relied on exporting oil and agricultural products, especially rice. Increasingly now its exports are moving towards less labour-intensive, more capital-intensive goods. There are also a few signs now that the composition of its exports is moving towards technology-intensive goods. Through each of these different phases global integration has remained part of China's reform story, and also part of the story of demand for global resources. Very briefly, that is the story of the China boom.

Let me just add here that China is one of the richest countries in terms of natural resource endowments, coal, other minerals, etc. But it's just not big enough. So in the past ten years, the import dependency ratio (defined as the ratio of imports to domestic consumption) for key commodities, oil, plutonium, natural gas, and even coal, has been on the rise. China has 47 per cent of the global reserves of coal, but it now needs to import it, and in 2009 China became a net importer of coal for the very first time. And China's strong demand for these commodities has had a very direct impact on global commodity markets and global commodity prices.

Figure 8 considers the question of how long the China boom will last. This is a very important question, especially for foreign companies, and mining companies in particular. It looks as if the boom is easing off now, with metal prices easing – the price for iron ore has been dropping steadily this year (2014) and is now below US$100 a tonne, though overall metal prices are still relatively high. On the other hand agricultural prices continue to be quite strong, a very important consideration for countries like New Zealand and to some extent Canada, Brazil and Australia that partly rely on agricultural exports. By the way, the rise in agricultural prices during the past decade is against the pattern of the past century, when the terms of trade for agriculture gradually deteriorated against manufactured goods at an annual rate of something like 0.5 per cent. So the strong agricultural prices of the last decade have really been unique, and help explain partly why the New Zealand and Australian economies have been doing well.

But back to the question of how long the boom in China will last. There are two major theories about this, and about the determination of future resource intensities. The first one is about leapfrogging in terms of technology catch-up under the pressure of environmental concerns, concerns about environmental degradation, and the task of rebalancing China's domestic economy. According to this theory

China may currently be embarking out of necessity on some kind of new path to industrialisation through a more rapid pace of technological advancement, since it cannot just follow the traditional way of doing things with 1.3 billion people entering modernity. There are certain constraints relating to this theory but I don't have time to consider them now.

Figure 8: Resource intensive growth and underpricing of resources

- How resource intensive will Chinese growth be and how long will the boom last?
    - Theories of leapfrogging and consumer preferences in determining resource intensities in development (per capita income, urbanisation, infrastructure, residential buildings, transportation, automobile penetration, industrialisation, trade and regional gaps)
    - continued increases in energy demand and CO_2 emissions without changes in energy efficiency and energy supply structure in the new phase of growth and development
- What are the implications of underpricing of natural resources (relative to social cost)?
    - reduction of the prices of investment goods leading to a higher ratio of investment to consumption
    - excessive natural resource use

The second theory is the consumer preferences theory. According to this theory, consumers change their preferences in consumer goods, with knock-on effects on resource demand and growth. In China's case consumers' demands have changed during the past few decades from sewing machines and bicycles to refrigerators and washing machines, and now to automobiles, residential goods, etc. In per capita terms Chinese consumers are still below the world average when it comes to resource demand, and multiplying by 1.3 billion people, you can see the scale of potential demand on resources. So the question of how long China's boom will last may depend in part on which of these two theories – leapfrogging to new technologies versus growing consumer demand – turn out to be applicable.

In any event it seems that the old key drivers for growth discussed earlier will continue to power on, even when facing constraints and the imperative of rebalancing. In particular they will continue to drive up energy demand and CO_2 emissions unless there are changes in two key fields: energy efficiency and the energy supply structure.

Let me say something about these two concepts. Energy efficiency is very important. It can be defined as the total energy consumed in production and consumption divided by total output. By this definition China has been doing quite well over the past ten to twenty years. Of course there is still a lot of inefficiency in utilising energy. There is the whole issue of China's energy supply structure, the composition of the country's energy supplies. There is tremendous pressure on China now since the country is still heavily reliant on coal.

One issue in this respect is energy pricing. Overall China's natural resources are still underpriced. So what are the implications of this underpricing? It is certainly an important factor in determining energy efficiencies and energy intensities in production, consumption and trade. In a way this problem of underpricing is a legacy of central planning. What do I mean by that? Well, during the past thirty years the commodity markets in China have been almost completely liberalised, with almost all commodity transactions being done through the market. However the factor market, including the financial market, the capital market, the labour market and – importantly in this context – the resource market, has somehow been left unreformed.

This lack of reform has basically resulted in the phenomenon of underpricing. What have the consequences been? Number one, importantly, is a reduction in the price of investment goods. That can lead to a higher ratio of investment to consumption. This is a demand side story. On the demand side there are three things to consider – investment, consumption and exports. In the past thirty years China has mainly relied on capital and on exports, and less on consumption. What is the explanation for that? The explanation is that resources are underpriced. When you have underpriced resources, what do you do? You engage in excessive use of the resources, and for any given output use up more resources, more energy. So this has to be changed, and can be changed through market-orientated reform, especially market-oriented reform of the factor market, including the energy market.

The second consequence of underpricing is its impact on the environment, which is very much linked to the overuse of resources because energy intensity is directly linked to carbon emissions. So the carbon intensity of growth and the environmental impact of growth is very much linked to the issue of underpricing of energy and resources. For China now it seems to me that there is a new concept to consider. Traditionally we have used the concept of physical capital, while increasingly people talk about human capital, and again social capital, and in the past couple of decades natural capital, which relates to ecology, the ecological system, etc. But now people are starting to talk about something new – environmental capital. Certain calculations can be made with respect to environmental capital, for example that one tonne of CO_2 emissions will lead to something like a US$20 loss of environmental capital.[1] A new concept like this becomes very important in discussing the issues relating to changes in energy intensity, carbon intensity and the consequent impact on the environment and climate change.

---

1   K. Arrow, P. Dasgupta, L. Goulder, G. Daily, P. Ehrlich, G. Heal, S. Levin, K. Maler, S. Schneider, D. Starrett and B. Walker, 'Are We Consuming Too Much?', *Journal of Economic Perspectives*, Vol. 18, No. 3 (2004), pp. 147–172.

Associate Professor Ligang Song from the ANU talking about natural resource pricing

Speakers have already mentioned today how bad the environment is in China now with respect to soil, water, air, deforestation, etc. Environmental degradation in China is creating enormous costs to society. These costs can be a necessary part of growing up, of rapid growth, but somehow the costs are increasing to the extent that they are triggering the government and local communities into saying 'we have got to do something about it'. This process is also related to what is called the Kuznets environmental U-curve (named after the economist Simon Kuznets, who originally postulated that income inequality tends to get worse with modern economic growth until average incomes reach a certain point, after which, things start to improve).

The big issue for China is whether with an annual average per capita income of US$8000 the country can start to tackle the environmental issue head-on. The Kuznets curve theory tells us that, according to past experience, a country won't deal with the environment effectively until its population has reached a certain level of per capita income. Thereafter the pollution of its air and its environment can peak and then start to come down. The theory does not just apply to China: it applies to all the later comers, whether they do something early on or wait for their per capita incomes to reach a certain level. China has probably not yet reached the peak point yet, but is already taking action to deal with its environment, out of necessity and concern for people's health. The World Bank has estimated that the social cost of China's environmental degradation amounts to about 10 per cent of its GDP. You know, an economy grows and its GDP figures go up but you can see what cost is behind that.

With respect to carbon emissions, most projections show that emissions will peak around 2025 to 2030, in another fifteen years or so, and given the situation right now, the task ahead is clearly enormous. It is basically related to the coal question. As I mentioned earlier, China still has vast coal reserves, and coal is relatively cheap there. So the key question with regard to reaching target peak levels of carbon emissions is very much related to the peak level of coal use. So when can China reach the peak level of coal use? Analysts are saying 'we will try do so as early as we can', but while that may be the intention the question is how. Later on, not now but probably in a few years' time, the government's intention is to cap coal use, and that will be compulsory.

Another hope is for radical change in energy consumption, finding alternatives to the dominant role now played by coal (which in 2013 constituted 66 per cent of the total energy consumption in China). So what are the alternatives? Petroleum, oil and gas are some. People are now forecasting that the age of coal is over in China, and that China is embracing the age of gas. But like coal and oil, gas is non-renewable. So there is a further task ahead, that of identifying renewable sources of energy. The government in China is massively investing in developing environmentally friendly technology – for harnessing wind and solar energy, etc.

Carbon leakage is a big issue for China right now. There are two dimensions to this, international and national. Usually people talk about the international dimension of carbon leakage, in reference to the fact that when countries develop they move their dirty industries offshore, to poor countries that have less stringent environmental regulations. For China though there is also a national dimension, for as its rising coastal regions' regulations become more stringent firms are moving inland, taking advantage of low costs of production there because of the income differences between different regions. Therefore the leakage will go on being huge if industries keep moving away from China, or from coastal China to the inland regions. International agencies as well as the Chinese government are very much concerned about what is to be done about carbon leakage in China, but yet to work out appropriate solutions to the problem.

Finally, there is the question of how environmental and resource reforms relate to SOE reform, or more broadly, to enterprise system reform in China. These are actually very much inter-related. We have been talking about the rebalancing of the Chinese economy, and one key component of this will be to improve resource allocation to be able to increase efficiency both at the macro and the micro levels. At both levels, efficiency is the issue. David Shambaugh has mentioned diminishing returns. With respect to SOEs, diminishing returns are currently evident on many fronts. For example, asset shares of SOEs are far higher than output shares. In recent years industrial capital-output ratios have been rising, highlighting inefficiencies in utilising capital as well as inefficiencies caused by monopolies, rent-seeking, etc.

If all these issues, as identified by economists, are gradually dealt with through deepened market-oriented reforms, China can increase energy efficiency on a tremendous scale. In fact, an early work by the International Energy Agency (IEA) shows that full-cost pricing of energy could reduce China's total energy consumption by 9 per cent. That's tremendous. So market reform with a focus on SOE reform and on removing barriers to market entry and exit can determine both the pace and the manner of industrialisation, with a move from the old pattern of industrialisation towards a new pattern with new forms of technology and investment carried out by the most efficient and productive firms. Ideally these new forms of technology and investment will be less energy intensive and less emission intensive, with enterprise system reform playing a very important role in achieving China's energy efficiency targets as well as its goals of low-carbon growth. This reform agenda is a key part of the reform strategy as laid out by the Third Plenum of the 18th Communist Party Central Committee.[2]

---

2   R. Garnaut, L. Song and F. Cai, 2014, 'Reform and China's long-term growth and development', Chapter 1 in L. Song, R. Garnaut, and F. Cai, eds, *Deepening Reform for China's Long-term Growth and Development* (Canberra: The Australian National University Press, 2014) pp. 3–26.

PART THREE
INTERNATIONAL AND REGIONAL IMPLICATIONS, INCLUDING FOR NEW ZEALAND

Although the Third Plenum did not address foreign policy issues as such, it met at a time when the contours and conduct of Chinese foreign policy appeared to be changing, with Chinese leaders apparently taking a more assertive approach to regional issues, including territorial disputes, and adhering less than before to Deng Xiaoping's advice that for the time being China should keep a low profile (tao guang yang hui, 韬光养晦). *Professor Zhai Kun discusses here the dilemmas facing President Xi Jinping, how China's rapid economic growth is affecting its conduct of foreign policy, and what this may mean for New Zealand as a potentially attractive partner for China in the Asia-Pacific region.*

Chinese Foreign Policy in the Light of the Third Plenum, with Special Reference to New Zealand

Zhai Kun

My topic will be Chinese foreign policy in the light of the Third Plenum with special reference to New Zealand. It is very hard for someone who is Chinese to speak about Chinese foreign policy. Sometimes it is not so easy as a Chinese to explain one's own country's foreign policy. You have often heard official or diplomatic presentations on the subject; I want to speak about it as a scholar.

I want to tell a story in four parts. The first part is 'Xi' foreign policy, 'X' meaning Xi Jinping, 'i' meaning first – Xi's first term in office, referring to the first five years of Xi's foreign policy. The second part is the dilemma of China's rise. Everyone has noticed the rise of China but no one has noticed the dilemma implicit in it. The third part is about how to explain this dilemma; how China's leaders handle China's complicated foreign policy – what their methodology is. I call it China's foreign policy dialectics. The final part of the story is about New Zealand and where its position is on the Chinese foreign policy map. You may find it very interesting that right now there is no clear position for New Zealand on the map. I want to find a position for you.

So the first part – Xi foreign policy. The first point to make in this regard is that the foreign policy of China's new government has been carried out for just eighteen months to date. Considering that the government will have two terms amounting to ten years in all, it may be too early to review China's foreign policy because it just the beginning. Mr Xi Jinping was Vice-President for five years (2007–12) and will now be President for ten years (2012–22). He communicated with President Bush and now communicates with President Obama, while post-Obama he will communicate with Obama's successor, perhaps Hillary Clinton. In China scholars frequently make the point that President Xi must be very patient because he still has eight years to go, while President Obama only has two and a half years to go. That is why only a few months is too short a time to reveal the direction of President Xi's foreign policy.

The second point is that every president in China has his own concept of foreign policy. Under former President Hu Jintao over the ten-year period 2002–12 the terms 'harmonious world' and 'harmonious society' were often seen, but now you seldom hear them. So what do we hear now? We hear the phrases 'community of shared destiny' and 'China dream'. Everybody knows the phrases, but what do they mean? The 'community of shared destiny' means that President Xi wants to seek a shared or common identity with the whole world. But where is China going? What is the goal of China's foreign policy? What is the China dream, the two-hundred-year-old dream? It means China's great recovery. That is very clear.

The third point is about China's foreign policy. The first issue here is the references now being made to 'a new type of great power relationship'. This refers to the relationships between China and the United States, China and Russia, China and the European Union, etc. I want to say here that President Xi wants to challenge the view expressed by Western scholars that China is 'a red country' and 'a hegemonic power'. The new type of great power relationship between China and the US is a very interesting framework in which President Xi wants equality with the US. You know, equality is a common goal for all the countries in the world when they communicate with the US. But I don't think the US has accepted that equality, because whereas we customarily use the term 'state' or 'country' for ourselves, for itself the US uses the term 'great power'. The US is a great power; China is just a country. That's unequal. President Xi's call for the two to be equal requires a re-evaluation by both Chinese and American scholars.

But relations between China and Russia are very good. There are two reasons for this. The first is that without stable relations between China and Russia there will be no stability for other neighbouring countries. The second reason is perhaps the Obama administration's strategic 'rebalance' in the Asia-Pacific region. China feels this is a threat, and according to realist theory this in turn makes more cooperation between China and Russia very necessary.

And under President Xi's leadership China's relations with European countries are getting better. Xi just finished a visit to Europe and Premier Li Keqiang also just finished a trip there. Relations are improving, especially with the German Chancellor Angela Merkel, who is very interesting. (I have heard the following joke. Why do Europe and especially Germany want to develop better relations with China? Because China has no intention and no capacity to know what Chancellor Merkel said on her mobile phone.)

The second issue relating to China's foreign policy is to do with China's own neighbourhood. 'Neighbourhood first' has always been a principle of China's foreign policy. There are two frameworks here. One is the Silk Road to the west of China – Central Asia, Russia and various other countries. The other is the maritime economic road to Southeast Asia, and perhaps also to the South Pacific island countries and New Zealand. It's an economic road – under this second framework there are a lot of approaches, like FTAs (free trade agreements), investment, infrastructure development and construction, so there is constant connectivity.

Another concept, the new Asian security concept, is China's, perhaps President Xi Jinping's concept of how to create security in Asia. Four terms are very important in this respect. The first is common security; the second is cooperative security; the third is comprehensive security; and the last is sustainable security. China likes to use the term 'sustainable economic development', and we also use the term 'sustainable' to describe security. In this context there have been a lot of problems recently with neighbouring countries of China, especially Japan, the Philippines, Vietnam and perhaps Myanmar and even North Korea. I will come back to the reasons for these a bit later on.

Finally, China's relations with developing countries. There are two terms in Chinese, *yi* 义 and *li* 利. *Yi* means morality and *li* means interest. I recall a speaker mentioning morality earlier today. Many developing countries believe China is quite an economic animal, just as Japan used to be, and President Xi has noted this. He wants to promote the right approach to morality and interest, with more morality than interest. So Xi has done a lot of things in support of multilateral organisations, including the United Nations, APEC (the Asia-Pacific Economic Cooperation forum) and others. The key words here are 'responsibility' and 'public goods' as demanded by the rest of the world. So China has given a lot of money for example to disaster relief in the Asia-Pacific region. There is also the good example of cooperation between China and New Zealand with respect to foreign aid to the Cook Islands for a water project.

So that is the whole map of Chinese foreign policy. But where is New Zealand? It is not a great power, nor a developing country, nor one of China's neighbours. Perhaps there is a role for New Zealand working with China in multilateral forums, and I'll come back to that later.

The second part of my story today is about how we explain Chinese foreign policy in the current situation. On the one hand you can see China rising. On the other hand you can see a lot of problems, especially in China's disputes with Japan and some Southeast Asian countries. I call this situation a rising dilemma. There are a lot of constraints and limitations on the whole process of China's rise. There are two factors in particular. The first is structural, and concerns the contributions and constraints entailed in China being the world's number two power. The second is China's economic ranking as the world's number two economy. In China there is a debate about these two factors. Does being the second largest economic power equate with being the second strongest power more comprehensively? Most Chinese don't believe that China is number two in comprehensive terms. Unfortunately the rest of the world disagrees, and believes that China is already number two

Professor Zhai Kun from the China Institutes of Contemporary International Relations talking about President Xi Jinping's foreign policy, with (seated from left) Professor Robert Ayson from Victoria University of Wellington, Dr Li-gang Liu from ANZ Bank, Mr Cameron Bagrie from ANZ Bank and Dr Marc Lanteigne from Victoria University of Wellington

The chair of panel 3, Professor Robert Ayson

comprehensively, not just economically.

So that's the trouble, and the origin of our dilemma. At the upper level there is the United States as number one, and under the US there are many other countries. China is regarded as a challenger to the current structure. That's why the US is adjusting its strategy towards China. But what good will come from being the world's number two power? China will contribute to the world economy like the US and other states, including New Zealand. China will evolve from a weaker to a stronger player, and China will be a new shaper of our living environment. Still there is a dilemma about how far at this stage China's authority and influence can reasonably be expected to reach.

There is another factor, too – the strategic factor. We are in a new world of proactive diplomacy. Our Foreign Minister Wang Yi has described the foreign policy of China's new leadership as proactive. What is the response from China's neighbours and the US? It is also proactive. That is why words like 'assertive' are being used to describe China's foreign policy, and why there have been some strong responses to it from China's neighbours. This is the strategic factor involved in describing China's rising dilemma. What is the way to break through this dilemma? I think it is mutual adaptation. China always advocates win-win. So how can we achieve a win-win situation? Adapting to each other may be the only way.

The third part of my story is about how to understand China's foreign policy from its roots. According to the current situation there are some contributions and some constraints, some complexity and some confusion when it comes to understanding China's foreign policy. How do China's top leaders manage so many things? In analysing this we must use the term China's foreign policy dialectics.

Western theory or traditional Chinese theory cannot explain the current thinking of China's top leaders. Only dialectics can. For China's new leaders, how to balance so many different things is an art. There are several points to make about this. First, President Xi and Premier Li were born in the fifties of the last century, and the common characteristic of their leadership is working hard. They were proved by a hard life, know how to deal with a hard life, and work very hard. This is the characteristic of their generation. Xi is not Mao, not Deng Xiaoping, not Hu Jintao. Xi is himself, but all the elements of former leaders can be found in him. He also has a very strong team. For example, Foreign Minister Wang Yi is very smart and knows his work very well. And one thing that's very new is that the top leaders pay a lot of attention to Chinese think-tanks in universities, and sometimes to think-tanks like ours (the China Institutes of Contemporary International Relations).

Second, there is the question of past versus future. In the past China had a certain position, conveyed a certain image; in the future what will these be? Third, there is the question of development versus security. Development is the priority of China's foreign policy but the security issue is increasing, and domestic emotions regarding security are increasing too. So China must show bottom-line thinking and add it to the idea of peaceful development, this bottom-line thinking being that we must avoid conflict with our own strength.

All the speakers today have argued that managing the Chinese economy and society is very complex work; but the logic and theory relating to domestic issues are different to those relating to external affairs. So it is a very tough task for the Chinese leadership to balance the management of domestic and external issues. To do so they use soft and hard approaches, soft words and hard means. Over the past ten years Chinese leaders may have been softer but right now they are harder than before. There are so many things for them to deal with in a country of 1.3 billion people, so many issues, that it is very difficult for them to find the right focus.

The last part of my story is about New Zealand. This is a question that I think everybody is interested in. First, I think Chinese love New Zealand, for two reasons. The first is that China is a great power or a big country, while New Zealand is a small country. So we find it is very interesting that we can develop very good relations with New Zealand – the FTA (the 2004 New Zealand-China Free Trade Agreement) and the 'four firsts' in New Zealand-China relations. But the other thing is the idea of *xiaoguo guamin* (小国寡民 'a small country with few people'), which was originally a Daoist idea – not Confucian but Daoist. The China dream is for China to be a great power; but another dream is of a *xiaoguo guamin*, a small country with a few people. The Chinese all like this. That's why so many Chinese people come to New Zealand to visit and to live.

President Xi Jinping will visit New Zealand in November 2014, before or after visiting Australia and attending the G20 summit.[1] At that time I think he will discover New Zealand's importance as a global and regional cooperation partner for China. For example, New Zealand is a member of the TPP (Trans-Pacific Partnership) and the RCEP (Regional Comprehensive Economic Partnership) negotiations. The RCEP and the TPP are currently the subject of a big debate in China. How and whether China will attempt to join the TPP and how to improve the RCEP are real problems. But we can learn from New Zealand and we can share some information with New Zealand. The China-New Zealand FTA is a mid-level free trade agreement, between a low-level FTA and a high-level FTA. So New Zealand is a very good ladder for China to use to enter the Asia-Pacific economy and promote a new balance in the Asia-Pacific region.

This is a new position for New Zealand, and New Zealand is a new land for China to develop relations with. It may be a very important point at which China can break through its rising dilemma.

---

1   G20 or Group of Twenty is the forum for the governments and central bank governors of the world's twenty major economies – ed.

ANZ's Chief Economist for Greater China, Dr Li-Gang Liu, takes the view here that many positive and concrete policy reforms have come from the Third Plenum, and predicts that in six years' time China's consumption market could be the second-largest in the world after the United States', even without taking into account the impact of current reforms. In his opinion this growth, as well as growth in outward Chinese investment, will be two major characteristics of China's involvement in the Asia-Pacific in the years to come. New Zealand should not, however, be overly concerned about being too economically dependent on China, as it will be well-placed to diversify its export markets as economic growth in more traditional markets improves.

The Impact of the Third Plenum and Other Recent Policy Initiatives on the Asia-Pacific Region

Li-Gang Liu

In my presentation I shall try to summarise China's Third Plenum and then tease out its key reforms – economic, population and financial reforms. I will also talk a bit about an emerging trend in China, that is, China's rising consumption. From that point on, I will talk about the implications for the Asia-Pacific region including New Zealand.

For the Third Plenum, I think it's very easy to summarise it into 'three reforms' and 'two institutions'. There are three very important reform directions. First of all, for the first time the Chinese Communist Party has given the markets a decisive role in allocating resources. In the past, if you read Party documents, the markets only played a supporting role.

The second very important reform is that for the first time the Party has given equal weight or status to China's state-owned enterprises and privately-owned enterprises. Over the last few years, there were a lot of complaints that the foreign direct investment environment in China was deteriorating. Chinese private firms had very little room to grow, and it is hoped that this new policy will encourage rapid private-sector development.

The third important reform is some sort of legal independence or centralisation. We don't want to over-interpret this – this is in no way comparable to western legal independence. Basically, the central government has seen a lot of corruption. If it can centralise the court system, local government will have less influence on or interfere less in local court cases and corruption could be somewhat contained.

In addition, and in distinction to previous Party plenums, two new institutions have been set up. The first is the so-called National Security Council. A lot of people came to identify this with the ADIZ (Air Defence Identification Zone) set up by China in the East China Sea in November 2013. In fact, this National Security Council should have a very similar role to comparable institutions in other countries, especially the National Security Council in the United States. It will coordinate China's defence, economic and diplomatic policies. It will be responsible for China's food security, energy security, and even financial stability. The second new institution is, I think, more important. The previous government in China talked about reforms for many years but did not take concrete reform actions. The main reason is that there was not an institution that could think about China's reform in a comprehensive way. It is hoped that the new Central Leading Group for Comprehensively Deepening Reform can play that role. In the future, reforms can be thought out first by this institution, then the State Council and ministries can implement them. So in that sense I believe this Third Plenum reform document will have some far-reaching implications for China over the next five to ten years.

We economists do try to interpret the Plenum documents and tease out the implications for reform in different areas in the future. In certain areas, reform has already been quite decisive. For example, before the sixty-paragraph Decision of the Third Plenum was released, a lot of people thought that population policy would not be changed. But in one sentence in the document, young couples are allowed to have two children. In banking and financial reform, it is very clear that China will engage in interest rate liberalisation and capital account opening, and will also build up bond markets so that China can have a reasonable yield curve. Also, for state-owned enterprise (SOE) reform, it is very clear that China's SOEs should have diversified ownership going forward. In fact, CITIC Group[1] will be the first SOE to list in Hong Kong. That means its state ownership will be very much diluted from the current almost 100 per cent to probably around 50 per cent.

So you can see that there is indeed a lot of very detailed discussion in the Decision on how China's reforms should be done. In SOE reform, the Decision also requires SOEs to pay the state an annual dividend equivalent to at least 30 per cent of profits by 2020, and so again you can see that some of the reform is actually rather decisive.

On fiscal policy, we have seen a lot of over-indebtedness in local governments; however, there does exist one very important policy to solve that. From now on, China's local government can issue bonds for infrastructure financing purposes. This will help establish a US-style municipal bond market. As we know, given

---

1   A very large state-owned investment company set up in 1979 by the well-known businessman Rong Yiren with encouragement from Deng Xiaoping. It gets its acronym from its former name in English, the China International Trust and Investment Corporation – ed.

China's huge size there are very few bureaucrats to monitor local government. In the future, I think the bond market will be a very good monitoring mechanism. That is, if Chinese local governments issue debt, they will have to open up their books for rating agencies. Rating agencies can analyse their expenditure and revenue, and so the finances of local governments will become more transparent than before.

With regard to market monitoring, local People's Congresses will eventually be able to monitor local government finances. In the future, if a local government were to issue a bond for building a white elephant project, People's Congress members at the local level could perhaps reject it. We can see that even though what we are talking about is an economic policy, it will have major political implications for China. That is, from now on taxpayers will be able to monitor local Chinese governments. Indeed, these are detailed policy reforms that could bring about far-reaching changes in China.

I want to make one further point, which is about land reform. The Plenum Decision did not make a radical change with regard to land reform, but from now on, I think, farmers' land-lease titles will be firmed up. There are experiments under way enabling them to use land-lease titles as collateral to borrow from the banking system. You can see this as a form of de facto wealth transfer, shifting wealth from the state to the farmers. By doing this China could create a significant wealth effect in its rural sector, and thus help China's economic rebalancing, as it would have a major implication for China's consumption.

Dr Li-Gang Liu talking about Third Plenum reforms, Asia and New Zealand

Now let me talk about consumption. We know that an imbalanced economic structure is very much the biggest problem facing the Chinese economy at this moment. Investment's share in GDP is close to 50 per cent, while consumption's share is 36 per cent. We do see some initial signs of economic structural change. In 2013, for example, China's tertiary sector exceeded its manufacturing sector as a proportion of GDP for the first time. That is an important structural change.

We also think that the previous government has laid the ground for fast consumption growth in China. For example, the western press has seldom mentioned the fact that China introduced universal medical care reform during the global financial crisis. In 2009 the government spent almost RMB600 billion to give most of the population a universal medical insurance package. At the moment, the package covers 96 per cent of the population. In the past, in the rural sector especially, farmers didn't have any medical coverage. The government hopes that this universal medical coverage will reduce precautionary savings among Chinese farmers. In addition, before the departure of the previous government the then Premier Wen Jiabao provided rural farmers with a minimum pension. In the past, Chinese farmers basically relied on their children for their retirement. These measures, together with the ongoing land-lease title reform, will help boost China's consumption. What's more, we have also seen rapid wage increases in China, which could do the same.

Let me give you some numbers to highlight why we think China's consumption is rising and will continue to rise at a very fast pace in the future. China currently has a 50 per cent national savings rate, the highest in the world. This is largely due to so-called precautionary savings, which are motivated by the need to meet costs relating to retirement, medical care, children's education and other purposes. We also know that China's consumption as a share of GDP is quite small now, equivalent to 36 per cent of GDP. But if you look at its actual size, it's not small at all. China's consumption is about US$3.3 trillion, the same size as Germany's GDP.

We think urbanisation will help boost China's consumption. If you look at the growth rate of consumption in urban and rural areas, you tend to see very fast growth in urban areas. Nowadays Chinese consumption patterns are changing in a way that is very similar to past changes in the West. That is, Chinese people tend to spend twice as much on durable goods as on necessities, while they spent equally on necessities and durable goods more than ten years ago. If you look at what they are spending on, the automobile is a major item of consumption expenditure. If you look at the ownership of durable goods per hundred households, the biggest growth area is the automobile.

Also, as I just mentioned, China's wages are rising at a very fast pace. The three biggest provinces in terms of GDP, Guangdong, Jiangsu and Shandong, have the fastest-growing minimum-wage and high-wage groups. At the moment the Chinese Academy of Social Sciences tends to define the middle class in China as those who have a household income of around RMB100–150,000 per year. Using this definition, the middle class in China constitutes about 15 per cent of the total number of urban households. Using some assumptions to project forward, we estimate that this share could rise to 45 per cent by 2020. How large will the consumption level then be? We believe that the consumption size of the middle class in China in 2020 could be US$9.3 trillion in PPP (purchasing power parity) terms. By 2020 China's total consumption could rise to around US$10.7 trillion, as against US$4.5 trillion in 2012, while total US consumption could be around US$16 trillion. So in six years' time, China's consumption market could be the second largest in the world.

So we talk about overdependence on China, but I think we are just seeing the initial signs of it. Going forward, New Zealand and the Asia-Pacific economy will become more dependent on the Chinese economy. But I would say don't worry. There's a very good theory from physics to explain why countries trade with each other. It's called the gravity model, and it can explain a country's trade behaviour very nicely. Economic size is one of the most important determinants in a trade relationship, but distance tends to weigh on the relationship. Per capita income is another very important factor. Hopefully the G3 economies (the economies of the US, Europe and Japan) will recover so that New Zealand's traditional markets will come back. New Zealand could then be in a perfect position to choose where to export. I don't think New Zealand should worry about its overdependence on the Chinese economy.

Finally let me talk about Asia very briefly. Figures 9 and 10 suggest that Chinese trade structure is changing. Before 2008, the so-called processing trade was dominant in China. Since 2008, China's ordinary imports have started to increase significantly. If you consider China's trade sophistication, you can see that ten years ago the share of manufacturing in China's total exports was about 60 per cent, while now it is more than 67 per cent. If we look at sophisticated export products in China's trade, we will see that nowadays China can produce almost anything that an OECD (Organisation for Economic Co-operation and Development) country or a European Union country can produce, suggesting that China's trade structure is changing very fast.

That's about the trade structure. Let's then look at the cost side. We know that in real terms the renminbi has been appreciating at a very fast pace over the last eight years, and has appreciated by about 30 per cent. More importantly, if you look at Chinese wages, statistics show that foreign-funded firms in China already have the highest wage rates in Asia. That's a reason why China is increasingly investing abroad. Ten years ago, China had only invested about US$10 billion overseas, while now its overseas investment is close to US$100 billion. FDI (foreign direct investment) into China, on the other hand, peaked in 2011 and has since been on a declining path.

In terms of China-ASEAN trade, ASEAN (Association of Southeast Asian Nations) states have plenty of natural resources and China has imported quite a

Figure 9: Processing trade is gradually moving to the back seat, while ordinary trade will become the key driver for rebalancing China's trade structure

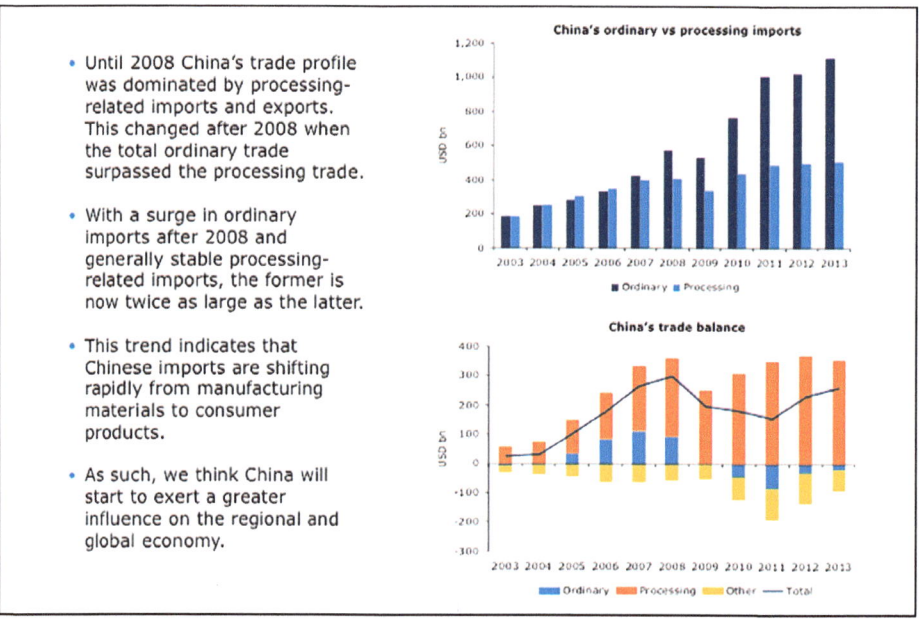

- Until 2008 China's trade profile was dominated by processing-related imports and exports. This changed after 2008 when the total ordinary trade surpassed the processing trade.

- With a surge in ordinary imports after 2008 and generally stable processing-related imports, the former is now twice as large as the latter.

- This trend indicates that Chinese imports are shifting rapidly from manufacturing materials to consumer products.

- As such, we think China will start to exert a greater influence on the regional and global economy.

Figure 10: China's trade sophistication has been gradually increasing

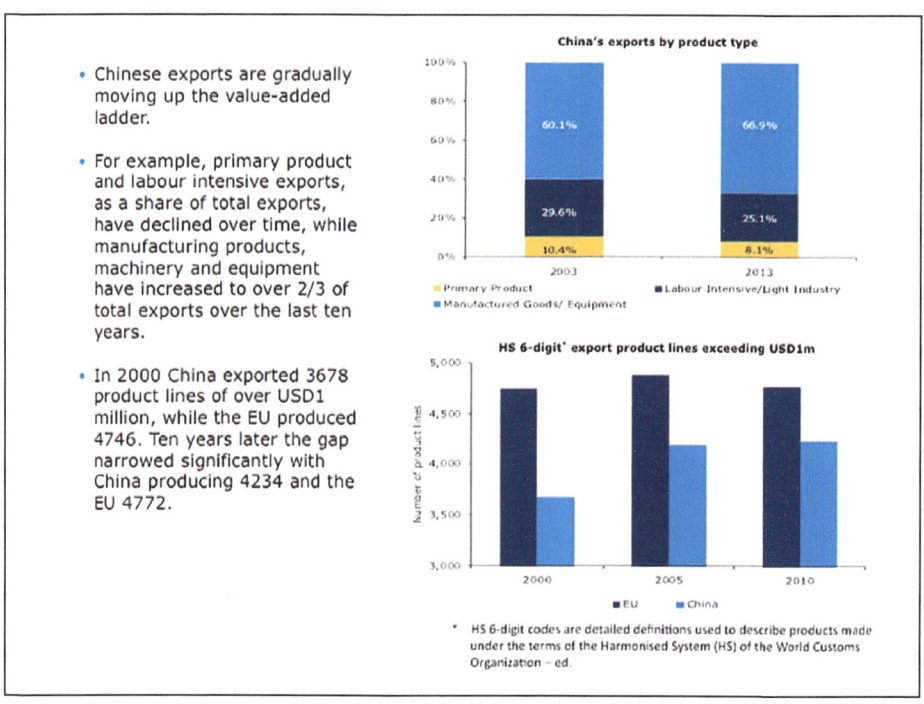

- Chinese exports are gradually moving up the value-added ladder.

- For example, primary product and labour intensive exports, as a share of total exports, have declined over time, while manufacturing products, machinery and equipment have increased to over 2/3 of total exports over the last ten years.

- In 2000 China exported 3678 product lines of over USD1 million, while the EU produced 4746. Ten years later the gap narrowed significantly with China producing 4234 and the EU 4772.

* HS 6-digit codes are detailed definitions used to describe products made under the terms of the Harmonised System (HS) of the World Customs Organization – ed.

lot. But in terms of manufacturing, there is a great deal of two-way trade. This means that the Asian production chain, led by advanced economies such as Japan, South Korea, Taiwan and increasingly China that invest in the region on the basis of labour costs and regional comparative advantage, is still working in East Asian trade.

Finally, I think the major implication for China's involvement in the Asia-Pacific region in the near future is the potential large outflow of capital. We have been talking about renminbi internationalisation – the Reserve Bank of New Zealand signed a bilateral swap arrangement with the People's Bank of China in 2011, and now we also have direct trading between the renminbi and the New Zealand dollar. We think the renminbi will first be used as a trade invoicing currency, and will then be used as a trade financing currency and eventually a foreign exchange reserve currency. Once China's capital markets become more open, we will see more renminbi-based investment in the Asia-Pacific. In this sense, going forward the Asian region will no longer rely on short-term volatile capital from the western economies. China's commitment to the region will be a stable source to boost regional infrastructure and longer-term investment. Indeed the new Asian Infrastructure Investment Bank is orientated towards that.

ANZ Bank's Chief Economist in New Zealand, Mr Cameron Bagrie, takes a closer look at New Zealand's trade relations with China, and sees plenty of room for optimism in a fast-changing economic environment. There are good grounds for optimism, he argues, provided New Zealand businesses figure out how to manage trading with China strategically, and with an eye on the fact that in the course of China's reforms the China market can change, sometimes quickly and unpredictably.

The Impact of the Third Plenum and Other Recent Policy Initiatives on New Zealand

Cameron Bagrie

I am going to try and keep this pretty short and succinct. It's not your normal economic-style presentation. It's a little bit more akin to a bit of speed dating, because what we are going to talk about is rockstars, boy bands, Kardashians, forestry, log trucks and probably Fonterra. So please try to keep up.[1]

I'm going to make three points. Point one: I want to have a quick chat about the rockstar economy and put in perspective what NZ Inc. is actually going through. The term rockstar, if you believe the press, was coined by an Australian economist who visited New Zealand in January this year (2014). Like all good Australians he pinched it from a New Zealand fellow. I know that for a fact because it was me that used the term in May 2013 with Bill English[2] at a budget lunch. Now when I used the term rockstar it was in a relative sense. New Zealand was looking okay because most other countries around the globe were looking pretty stuffed. So we were wearing one of the cleanest of all the dirty shirts. But right here and now New Zealand has really got a nice little economic hum under the bonnet. As such, interest rates are moving up, the New Zealand dollar is sort of strong – but there are good reasons for that.

But sometimes in this game you've got to step back and have a look at the underlying picture showing what New Zealand is going through. The New Zealand economy today is going through a fundamental economic transformation. In 2008 our economic model literally blew up. Pre-2008 we had a Freddy Mercury-style economy. We wanted it all and we wanted it now. Credit growth was growing at 10–15 per cent; asset prices the same. We had a very heavy build-up of leverage over

---

1 Mr Bagrie has asked us to note that since he spoke without notes, the odd term or phrase in his speech might have been different had his presentation originally been in written form – ed.
2 New Zealand's Deputy Prime Minister and Minister of Finance – ed.

a number of decades, such that in 2008 net external debt across New Zealand was 85 per cent of GDP in the red. The household savings rate was minus 6 cents and the current account was minus 9 per cent of GDP. That spelt a bit of an economic mess. And right here and now, some of those legacy issues have been partially addressed. The household savings rate has gone back to zero. It's gone from being dreadful to being poor. It's better than what it was. Net external debt has gone down to 65 per cent of GDP.

But here in New Zealand today we've still got a few legacy issues that need to be addressed. The flipside to legacy is opportunity. And at no time in the last fifty years has the medium-term landscape for New Zealand probably looked this strong. It's all built around, of course, the China connectivity story. Li-gang Liu has talked about the structural consumption story across the emerging market economies, including China – it's all built around New Zealand being the eighth wealthiest country around the globe in regard to natural resources on a per capita basis. Australia, 'the lucky country' – guess what, they are number eleven. We are wealthier than Australia. We are the wealthiest country in regard to renewables. We are long on food, Asia is short: connect the dots. So there's the opportunity landscape.

In between, New Zealand has to find 15,000 houses in Auckland, on top of 10,000 per year because of population growth. We've got to rebuild our second largest city, Christchurch, and of course we've got an overvalued New Zealand dollar to contend with. That is one hell of an economic undertaking. So where we sit today across New Zealand, even though we can focus on rockstar-status terminology, behind the scenes we see an economy that has still got tremendous frictions and tensions. But one of the keys to managing these frictions and tensions is to pull on the income-generating lever. When you've got a structurally impaired balance sheet and you have got to put money away for a rainy day and demographic pressures are around the corner, the more aggressively New Zealand pulls that income-generating lever – and the China part of the story is a big part of the equation – the more flexibility, the better space New Zealand is going to be in in five to ten years. Now that's really message number one.

Message number two: forestry trucks. Six months ago, forestry pricing went through the stratosphere. The forestry sector was booming, whole-milk powder prices were trading at about NZ$5000 a tonne, and last season (2013–14) Fonterra made an NZ$8.40 dairy payout.[3] So the farming sector was swimming in it. Move six months on and forestry prices have tanked, as we speak there are forestry gangs getting told to stop work, we've seen a 30 per cent fall in dairy prices, and the price action in the past couple of weeks has not been that flash, such that we now expect the dairy payout this coming season to be NZ$6.25.

---

3   That is, Fonterra's farmgate milk payout to its farmer shareholders was $8.40/kg MS (kilogram of milk solids) – ed.

Now the main reason behind these massive variations in prices has been – both at the top and the bottom (and we hope it's the bottom) – the connectivity with the Asian market. This has brought tremendous strength in regard to what we see in cross-commodity developments. But of course with rising connectivity New Zealand has become increasingly connected into the fast-growing Asian region, particularly China. China now accounts for around 23 per cent of our export goods so it's strategically important for NZ Inc.

But with rising connectivity come susceptibility and vulnerability. Because as the Chinese go through swings and roundabouts, they rock and roll, and we are going to have to swing to that tune as well. And what we are seeing at the moment is a bit of a reminder that China too will experience some adverse movements in some key markets, and New Zealand needs to be mindful of those swings and roundabouts. It is not a one-way traffic story. As we become connected into the fast-growing Asian region, particularly the likes of China, we have to be prepared to take the good with the bad. Because commodity prices, and we are a big commodity producer, go through peaks and troughs. So message number two is really about thinking, not just about connectivity, and about the strategic importance of the China market, but about how we manage some of the risks surrounding those opportunities.

Message three: really a look at what I consider to be the most important point in regard to where NZ Inc. is going in relation to Asia and China connectivity over the coming few years. New Zealanders sometimes I think need to be a little realistic. We are a nation of 4.4 million people. We've got free trade agreements either in place or pending with about 4 billion. There is of course a fast-growing China market, which we have heard a lot about the opportunities in today. Look, I'm in no doubt that the opportunity side of the ledger for NZ Inc. is taken care of. That one is baked into the economic story. The question marks I have about NZ Inc. are about the outright execution around those opportunities. And I'm just going to give you a couple of examples or hints, things that I have noticed over the past couple of years that give me an awful lot of hope or reason for optimism in regard to the NZ Inc. story.

If I go back to three years ago, and if I'd have looked through a Fonterra presentation or in fact listened to a Fonterra presentation, it was generally very long on how much milk China was going to need. And to be honest if 150 famers listened to that presentation, after the presentation they'd go have their cup of tea and a biscuit and they would talk about the three 'B's, which is the bach, the boat and the BMW, because the story generally speaking just didn't really resonate. Three years on – and of course Fonterra, which was a bellwether for NZ Inc., has had a few issues and we need to acknowledge those – three years on if you ever look at a presentation today coming out of Fonterra, they've got their six to seven key strategic prongs, they've got their three 'V's – value, volume, velocity – and they've got a strategic plan all built around executable modules in regard to where they are going.

Mr Cameron Bagrie talking about New Zealand and the China market

So the conversations we are having today have got far more of a strategic, executable edge; and when the big guys at the top are starting to convey execution-style dynamics over opportunity-style dynamics, that fundamentally changes the conversations down at the farmer level. Because all of a sudden they start to think about buying into the story as opposed to going away thinking about their three 'B's. If you have a look at Fonterra, they've now got someone who is Asian, who is based in Asia (in Singapore) on their board. And this is a New Zealand farmer-owned cooperative. This type of thing just doesn't happen by accident. And out of interest, how many other New Zealand primary producers have got someone of Asian descent on their board? The answer is very few. So we can talk a big game about how we are getting connected into this fast-growing Asian region, but quite often on some of the basics in regard to understanding the market – and the market up there is fundamentally different to our traditional markets – we are a little bit slow.

I could look at entities such as Auckland Airport. I have lost count over the past two years of how many events I've done in association with that entity. They're all built around flying down tourist operators from China. We did one last year in regard to a special Chinese charge card to explain to tourist operators to New Zealand, 'you need your facilities to be able to process this card, because the Chinese do not use Visa, so make sure your facilities can process this card as opposed to the other one'. These are the sorts of dynamics that I'm picking up time and time again. Blenheim. There's going to be 1.6 billion dollars' worth of wine exports in the coming twelve months because the grape harvest has just been an absolute rocket. In an ordinary environment, with our strategic vision I would say that would put a fair bit of pressure on grape prices over the next six to twelve months. Behind the scenes, that industry is very hopeful they've got the connections, they've got the strategic foresight and insight into that fast-growing Asian market to actually shift that product without putting pressure on the prices.

So the third message I've got here today is really taking the conversation away from opportunity. The opportunity side of the ledger is old school. We've been talking about opportunity for the past three or four years, that side of the equation I now think is very well baked in. The uncertainty, or the stuff we would like to see going forward, is whether we can take it to the next leg, demonstrate tangible executable-style strategies that are going to execute around those opportunities. That is the challenge for NZ Inc. going forward. From my perspective talking to people, I am very constructive, very upbeat on that message. Under the bonnet, behind the scenes, the message is about having tangible strategies in place in order to win in those markets. That message is really starting to sink in. It is not out in the public domain but it offers tremendous hope for NZ Inc. Because behind the scenes we've got a national balance sheet that is like the Kardashians and the boy bands. You can stomach it in the first instance but we'd just really like it to go away.

Policy trends reflected in the Third Plenum and subsequently suggest a stronger, more confident China both domestically and internationally. As China grows more assertive and China-US antagonisms increase, how should New Zealand place itself in regional affairs and in relation to the Asia-Pacific region's two great powers? Some have argued that New Zealand should draw closer to the United States; others that New Zealand should seek a greater equidistance between the United States and China; others still that New Zealand's current quiet diplomacy serves its interests quite well without modification. Dr Marc Lanteigne considers the shifting strategic landscape since the Third Plenum and looks at some responses and options, for the region and for New Zealand.

Sino-American Rivalries after the Plenum: New Zealand and Regional Responses

Marc Lanteigne

Although the Third Plenum primarily dealt with domestic reforms, the event took place within a difficult foreign policy atmosphere for China. Relations with the country's immediate neighbours, notably Japan, the Philippines and Vietnam, became more difficult by the end of 2013 due to ongoing maritime border disputes in the East and South China Seas. Foreign policy differences with the United States became more pronounced, while Chinese ties with large emerging economies, including Russia and India, began to improve. As the country's international interests began to expand, Beijing began to express more pronounced policy views on emerging conflict areas such as Afghanistan, Iraq, Mali, Ukraine and Syria. Closer to home, China's more diverse security concerns as well as the merger of domestic and global security threats prompted the creation at the Third Plenum of a CCP (Chinese Communist Party) National Security Council designed to create a specific nexus of information regarding strategic challenges on several levels. The Council, to be headed by Xi Jinping himself, underscored the growing importance of security on the Chinese government's agenda.

There have been several arguments made that China's strategic policies have entered into a new phase within the past five years as the country has developed more pronounced international interests and has become more comfortable with its rising great power status. These changes have been described in western circles as an overall more 'assertive' security policy on Beijing's part; yet this is a very broad term which begs greater understanding of how China's security interests have begun to diversify and in some cases have placed the country at increasing odds with policies of its immediate neighbours. At the same time, Chinese policies in the Western Pacific and South Pacific have also raised concerns in the United States and prompted much debate in New Zealand over China's emerging policy directions.

In the past half-decade, Beijing has first sought to better clarify its strategic interests closer to home, placing much new emphasis on maritime security, sea lanes of communication (SLoCs) and the protection of its trade and economic assets abroad. The PLA (People's Liberation Army) continues to be professionalised with a stronger interest in coastal defence but also in focusing on 'military operations other than war' (MOOTW). However, there has been much focus on how China's strategic policies in the Western Pacific have negatively overlapped with other East and Southeast Asian actors, specifically over the disputed sovereignty of the East and South China Seas. Issues such as fossil fuels, fishing, and the unilateral announcement in November 2013 of an ADIZ (Air Defence Identification Zone) in the East China Sea, including over areas also claimed by Japan, have all been cited as evidence that territorial friction in East Asia will continue to be a factor as Beijing's security policies continue to develop.

From an international viewpoint, China's security interests have also expanded well beyond the Asia-Pacific region. Beijing continues to develop stronger markets and trade partners in Africa, Europe and Latin America, and energy and resource diplomacy have marked much Chinese foreign policy in the developing world. Beijing is also engaging the developing world in ways that go beyond trade and aid matters. After many decades of being wary of the very concepts of peacekeeping and humanitarian intervention, seeing them as western concepts designed to maintain great power chauvinism, Beijing is now an active participant in UN peacekeeping around the world, with 2,188 active peacekeeping personnel supplied by China as of May of this year (2014). However, as has been recently seen in the cases of Syria and Crimea, there remain differences between China and the United States over the best solutions to humanitarian crises. Despite acceptance of the need for multilateral humanitarian intervention in some cases, there remains a lingering 'neo-Westphalian' foreign policy viewpoint which stresses the necessity of honouring the sanctity of state borders. However, Beijing is having to rethink its policies towards civil conflicts and collapsed states where governments are either severely weakened or altogether absent.

Since 2011, American policies in the Asia-Pacific have been dominated by the 'pivot' or 'rebalancing' policy which has underscored the ongoing importance of the region to US interests. American policymakers have sought to frame the rebalancing policy as a redistribution of assets to better favour the Pacific, especially given the role of that region as the anchor of the global economy since the onset of the global recession. However, it is interesting to note that the terms 'pivot' and 'rebalancing' have not been as well-used in the Chinese press as terms such as a 'return to Asia' (*chongfan Yazhou* 重返亚洲) policy. Although Washington has taken great pains to stress that its rebalancing policy, which has included improved security relations with Australia, Japan, the Philippines and Singapore, is not directed towards any given country, such assurances have not taken hold in Beijing, which despite its growing power retains a great sensitivity to perceived containment or 'encirclement' by the West.

Dr Marc Lanteigne talking about the regional implications of China's foreign policy

The rebalancing policy also has its share of detractors outside China, who view the rebalancing policy as 'full of sound and fury, signifying nothing'. Although the pivot policy has been criticised as an attempt at a de facto containment network, the structure of the pivot so far has been more akin to a set of tripwires and watchtowers, since there is little sign of an 'Asian NATO' emerging from the hub-and-spoke network of upgraded bilateral security relationships between Washington and its regional friends. There is also the question of whether the rebalancing policy to date has had a significant impact on China's growing security interests in East Asia. As well, the ongoing questions of the health of the US military budget have caused further obscurity. At present, despite repeated claims to the contrary, US strategic attention continues to be pushed elsewhere, including to the Middle East and Eastern Europe. There is the question, therefore, as to whether America's Asian allies are convinced that the US would be able to maintain its strategic presence in the region despite these other priorities.

As well, the rebalancing has been cited as a recognition of the growing economic importance of the region, especially in light of the current economic downturn. East Asia is now widely seen as the world's current economic engine, including not only China but also a Japan which has begun to regain its economic footing as well as several other Asian economies seeking to navigate international markets. The twelve-member TPP (Trans-Pacific Partnership), which began life as a nondescript, quadrilateral, small-state trade pact (which included New Zealand), is now commonly viewed, rightly or wrongly, as the economic arm of the rebalancing policy. Other Asian states, including Japan and Vietnam, are members of the agreement, with South Korea and Taiwan seriously weighing participation as well.

However, the Partnership's size and economic diversity have led to questions over the timeframe of an agreement, as evidenced for example by a growing rift among TPP members in June 2014 over (of all things) catfish inspection policies. There is also the fact that the second-largest economy in the world, China, remains outside that metaphorical smoke-filled negotiation room, with strong reservations in the US about allowing Beijing entry. This has placed New Zealand in a difficult position given the country's enthusiasm for the TPP as well as the growing percentage of New Zealand trade represented by China.

Finally, the rebalancing policy has been viewed as a means for the Obama administration to draw a line under the Middle East/Eurasia-focused strategies of the recent past, dominated by the Afghanistan and Iraq conflicts. However, the row of crises demanding American attention, including Libya, Mali, Syria, Ukraine and most recently (again) Iraq, have called into question whether Asia can truly remain at the top of US military priorities in the near future.

All of this calls forward the debate about what Sino-American relations in the Pacific will consist of in the coming years. Ideas such as 'spheres of influence', a G2 (US-China Group of Two), a 1914 scenario, and a rise in zero-sum policies have been regularly bandied around in policy discussions, but the reality is unlikely to fall under these convenient categories. There are many policy differences which could create further troubles in the bilateral relationship in the future, but no scenario is inevitable.

Although it has been commonplace to lump Australia's and New Zealand's China policies together, it can readily be argued that the two states are if anything starting to drift apart on the subject of how to address China's rise and American policies in the Pacific. Unlike New Zealand, there is little question regarding Australia's role in the rebalancing policy, ever since the then Prime Minister Julia Gillard agreed to host US Marines at Darwin in late 2011, prompting caustic comments in the Chinese press about archaic, cold war thinking on the part of the West. Recent Australian policies, including criticism of the ADIZ and warming relations between Canberra and Tokyo, have further strained relations between Australia and China and have placed their long-delayed bilateral free trade negotiations further in doubt.

Like New Zealand, Australia is seeking to improve economic ties with Beijing, but there is the question of whether Australia's strategic and economic policies towards China can be well reconciled. In the case of New Zealand, there is a greater tendency to view China as primarily an economic challenge, given the successes of the five-year-old Free Trade Agreement between New Zealand and China and the growing role of Chinese businesses in the New Zealand economy. Despite considerable progress in repairing US-New Zealand ties since the Wellington Declaration was signed in late 2010, it is unlikely that New Zealand will play the same role within the rebalancing policy as its neighbour.

Although the term has a negative connotation in some policy circles in Wellington, there should be a more open debate over whether New Zealand regional policy may have to adopt greater 'neutralism' as a result of its interests in maintaining robust links with both Beijing and Washington. This concept, referring to the peacetime practice of eschewing active engagement of blocs and developing a foreign policy based on non-alignment, may become more attractive given New Zealand's size and distinct geography and trade structure. Adding to the complexity of New Zealand's economic ties to the region is the free trade agreement (officially known as an Economic Cooperation Agreement) completed between Wellington and Taipei in July 2013, the first such agreement Taiwan has undertaken with a non-diplomatic partner.

The South Pacific has been another area where Chinese and Western policies have increasingly encountered each other, and much of the debate there is not over hard military power but rather the policies of aid and economic partnerships. When looking at Pacific security, there has been a tendency to view the region as a doughnut,[1] but to fully understand what role the greater Pacific will play in security developments and Sino-US relations, the South Pacific cannot be left out.

Although Australia remains far and away the largest assistance partner in the South Pacific, China in a short time has assumed the role of 'the alternative donor', due to its 'no-strings' approach to granting aid and assistance to Pacific Islands. This approach has had a great impact on some Pacific Island states, such as Fiji, which had been critical of Australian and New Zealand policies tying aid to governance issues. China's rapid appearance in the Pacific has raised questions about whether Beijing, Canberra and Wellington (and Washington) can develop as economic partners or competitors in the region. While Beijing has declined to join the Cairns Compact, which coordinates aid activities in the South Pacific, China has been warming to the idea of joint cooperation in some specific regional aid initiatives, including the China-New Zealand-Cook Islands waterworks project under way in Rarotonga.

To conclude, the 2014 RIMPAC (Rim of the Pacific Exercise) naval manoeuvres in Hawaii are also an important illustration of how strategic affairs in the Pacific

---

1   By this I mean that unlike East Asia the South Pacific is a region that suffers from weak regional organisations, and ones that do not connect the region well with either Asia or North America.

are changing. For the first time in thirty years, New Zealand naval vessels, led by HMNZS *Canterbury*, were permitted to dock at Pearl Harbour along with the other participating ships. At the same time, vessels from the PLA Navy, led by the Lanzhou-class destroyer *Haikou*, are also taking part in the RIMPAC 2014 operations. Although China's rise as a great power continues to dominate discussions about Asia-Pacific security, the question of which directions the region will go in the area of strategic relations is one which cannot be answered by only one or two voices.

Questions and Answers

During the Third Plenum conference there were several opportunities for those listening to presentations to put questions to the presenters. Here is a selection of the answers given to a variety of questions relating more or less directly to the Plenum and subsequent policy developments.

Did the 2013 Third Plenum just set the general tone for change?

David Shambaugh (*in answer to a question about whether the 2013 Third Plenum resembled the pathbreaking Third Plenum in 1978 in the sense that both Plenums opened the door to a new reform era rather than prescribing policies in detail*): Well, in fact if one goes back and looks at the outcomes of the '78 Third Plenum they weren't put down in a systematic, published form. We learnt about them only after the fact. Interestingly enough, many of the decisions taken then were very immediate. For example, the Chinese decided to normalise relations with the United States at that meeting, they decided to attack Vietnam – sorry, carry out a 'self-defence counter-attack' against Vietnam – as well as a few other very specific things. But they also launched the economic reforms, as you said.

So what we think of today as the 1978 Third Plenum is in some way retrospective, reading into the meeting the results of the last thirty years. We give it a lot of credit for kick-starting the reforms of the last thirty years, but in fact if we go back and analyse the meeting itself, that wasn't obvious at the time. I remember as an analyst working in the United States government – I was in the US intelligence community that year – we didn't pay particularly full attention to the Third Plenum at the time, though obviously in retrospect it was critical. We paid a lot of attention to the personnel changes at the meeting – Chen Yun, Deng Xiaoping, Li Xiannian, others taking power – but not so much its policy decisions.

So thirty years, even three years from now, we may look back differently. Meantime, as I say, we have to read the Plenum Decision over and over, because turns of phrase are important. But there is a lot of opacity in the documents. And I guess your question is, isn't that to be expected – broad parameters, broad initiatives, not a lot of detail? Yes, I suppose you are right. So we are waiting for the detail. It has been eight months now since the Plenum, and the State Council has not produced a single document about detailed implementation in any of these areas. Perhaps Christine has seen some in financial sector reform or other areas. So I think we still really have to wait and see what they are going to do. Maybe the Plenum decisions are indeed broad gauged, ambitious, but I am not persuaded. I want to see the details.

Professor Anne-Marie Brady putting a question to Professor David Shambaugh, with Professor Kerry Brown (right) looking on

Professor Anita Chan answering a question from the audience

Are China's problems today any worse than those of the United States?

David Shambaugh (*in answer to a question from one of the conference chairs,* **Anne-Marie Brady**, *about whether China's problems aren't comparable to those of the United States*): I am not going to dispute the fact that the United States has problems, we have lots of them, all societies do. But for all the failings of the United States, we have a separation of powers that works pretty well, although it does occasionally cause difficulties.

Anyway I don't want to get into a comparison between China and the US – it's like mixing apples and oranges. We are here to talk about China, and I stand by what I said. I think China's is a highly fragile society. I've been watching it my entire career; I have gone to and lived in China for 35 consecutive years, more than half of my life, and I've never seen it so stressed, so fragile, so angry, the party-state embattled and endangered for the reasons we've heard from Anita Chan and Stephen Noakes in particular. And I didn't have time in my own presentation to talk about what the Plenum had to say about other problems, state-owned enterprise reform or even legal reform or other areas.

So I think the topic for the conference, 'China at the crossroads', is very apt. China is really at a crossroads today for the reasons I and others have elaborated. I take the long view that the society has accomplished a great deal and deserves a lot of credit, but is at a series of junctures now that mean that if Chinese leaders don't take very fundamental decisions to loosen the political system they are not going to achieve the goals they want to achieve. The political system is, I would argue, a real impediment to everything that we have talked about, workers, civil society, property rights, (if I understood you correctly, Jonathan, you argue it's a good thing to have collective property rights, but I'm sorry, I come from a more libertarian perspective), state-owned enterprise reform. So the party-state monopoly over everything which is getting tighter and tighter not looser and looser is really the overarching challenge and impediment to China.

How is China today affected by Taiwan, and vice versa?

Kerry Brown (*in answer to a question about the possible influence on mainland China of Taiwan*): Taiwanese cultural influence in mainland China has been there since the 1980s. Remember the two Dengs, the Deng of the day and the Deng of the night? – Teresa Teng of the night, the great Taiwanese singer, and Deng Xiaoping of the day.[1] But the Taiwan President Ma Ying-jeou now has a 9 per cent popularity rating and so you have a very profound problem with what the future holds for Taiwan. The Economic Cooperation Framework Agreement that the Taiwanese signed with China in 2009 liberalised 570 tariffs with the mainland, and if you

---

1   Both have the same surname 邓 in Chinese – ed.

looked at it as a free trade agreement it was a good deal for Taiwan. But actually it has brought good and bad, because Taiwan is now in a sense overwhelmed by the economy in China, it's too dependent on it. The bubble of mainland China in Taiwan's economy has become all-encompassing. So the services agreement that was going to be signed this year was a big, big problem because public opinion in Taiwan was not keeping up with the government there, and there were huge protests in March and April.

When we talk about China's soft power, how should we define it?

David Shambaugh (*in answer to a question about soft power, and about whether soft power can be seen either as a means to change the world in one's image or as a means of getting a better press in the outside world*): I absolutely agree – there's a distinction to be made between public diplomacy and soft power. In Chinese the Chinese use the term 'external propaganda'; but what they call external propaganda every other country calls public diplomacy. We all have public diplomacy departments in our foreign ministries, and their job is to tell the world their government's interpretation of any situation. That's what the Chinese are doing. That's not soft power. Soft power, if you take the Joseph Nye definition, is societally driven, it's about universalization. If you have soft power you do not have sui generis, unique characteristics. Whatever characterises your society – your values, your economic and political systems, your popular culture, your high culture, your films, literature and intellectual life, travels. It travels outside your borders and resonates with others who are attracted to it – that's the magnetic pull of soft power. Public diplomacy, you're quite right, is a one-way state-led effort and that's what the Chinese are trying to do. They are trying to buy soft power through public diplomacy. Soft power doesn't work that way; you have earn soft power, and they are having great difficulty in doing so.

Anne-Marie Brady (*on the same question about soft power*): The objective for China's investment in 'foreign propaganda', to use the Chinese terminology, is to improve China's international image. The Chinese recognise that since 1989 they have had a really serious global image problem. So they are not trying to make anyone become like China, that's not the goal, although people do talk about the China model (and if a country like Fiji or Zimbabwe wants to learn the China model then it can get some advice on that), but what they really want to do is to improve global public opinion on China. And while it would be nice for them if people liked their political system, their society and so on, their main goal is actually to promote the strength of the Chinese economy. It is the core stated goal and has been since the early 1990s; and on that point, they are doing pretty well.

What if anything did the Third Plenum say about women?

Stephen Noakes: (*in answer to a question about the situation of women in China, and the fact that in politics today women 'just seem to be invisible'*): I don't recall anything specific about the status of women in the Plenum document itself, but I can say that there is most certainly a gender dimension to the development task in China; and to the extent that women's issues are pushed, the impetus for development programmes specifically seeking to address women's issues tends to come from international organisations rather than from domestic partners per se. The success of these programmes depends on how women's issues get pitched to potential sponsors and supervisors in the Chinese state.

Jonathan Unger (*on the same question, the situation of women in China*): The situation for women in China is not as bad as it is in a country like India or Pakistan, or other parts of the world; but the Chinese government is not particularly enlightened on women's issues – in fact quite the opposite. Women's representation in high level political positions is almost non-existent. You just take a look at who attended the 2013 Plenum of the Communist Party Central Committee; there are very few women at the higher levels. If you look lower, rather than treating women as equals, or taking affirmative action for women, most official agencies' regulations go against women. We are sitting here in a university – take university admission policies. Overall in China, in secondary schools women tend to do better than the men. But for most universities women have to score higher to get in – the universities actually announce this – than men do. The reason the universities give for this is that employers including public employers are biased against employing women – their excuse is that women will have children. So in accordance with that, the universities say, we will have to have a higher score for women entrants, we will deliberately favour men. And the national government does nothing about this. It is oblivious to this type of bias.

Do university exchange programmes improve intellectual freedom in China?

David Shambaugh (*in answer to a question about intellectual freedom in Chinese universities, and the degree to which exchange programmes with foreign universities have affected it*): One can respond to your question in either a current, static way or from a more dynamic longer term perspective. I was a student at a Chinese university thirty years ago, along with Professor Huang Xiaoming who is with us today. Anyone in a Chinese university thirty years ago or even earlier will remember the conformity and the lack of diversity of opinion in the classroom, and for that matter in books, libraries and general discourse. So compared to thirty years ago and the Third Plenum of that period, Chinese campuses today are remarkably open. I give lectures on a number of them with some frequency and I'm always stunned by the questions that one gets, and I'm sure conversations among Chinese students are remarkably diverse too. And that's a good thing.

The degree to which exchanges with the outside world have had a catalysing effect – that I don't really know, I suspect that is the case, but I would myself give more credit to domestic factors. So yes, on a longitudinal basis there has been a lot of progress compared to thirty years ago when the conformity and rigidity was extraordinary. Having said that, there is still a lot of conformity and rigidity. China's is still a university system that is primarily based on examinations in which rote memorisation gets you to do better on the exams. In fact in most subject areas that I am familiar with the questions on the exams are available beforehand. In fact the national *gao kao* 高考, the national entrance exam, is available beforehand – in other words you get the questions and the answers before you take the exam, and the responsibility of the exam taker is one of memorisation. The closer to verbatim memorisation of the answer you can get, the higher your score is.

So this is not a system that is based on essays or on research papers necessarily or on criticism and individual interpretations. This is still a heavily conformist system, and textbooks are still largely state approved. So yes, a lot of progress; but you have to link this to the innovation question I raised earlier. If China is to become a knowledge economy and truly become creative and move up the value chain, it's got to really start with the higher education system, and also the pre-collegiate system. They've made a lot of progress, but the relationship between the political system, which is tightening, and the educational system is a key impediment to innovation, in my view, and they are not going to be able to innovate, create, win Nobel prizes, break out of the middle income trap unless they loosen the constraints on the higher education environment in particular. And this requires a loosening up of civil society and the whole political system.

Do Chinese construction companies enjoy monopolies?

Christine Wong (*in answer to a question about whether companies sometimes have a monopoly on both borrowing funds and securing contracts in sectors such as infrastructure development*): The answer is that I don't know if certain sectors are in it more than others. I would guess that this is a win-win kind of game for lots of actors involved. The SOEs can make money without doing anything. They go to the bank and borrow money, they re-lend it and earn a percentage in the process. There was a default a couple of weeks ago of a very large real estate company in I think Hangzhou. It turns out that this real estate company was very intimately linked to the municipal government, that it had borrowed billions that it was defaulting on, and that the money came from four very large SOEs who now find themselves with IOUs that aren't coming back. It's not clear what the resolution will be, but up until now every case has been bailed out eventually by somebody.

Questions and Answers

Is Chinese foreign policy still one of non-interference?

Zhai Kun (*in answer to questions about China's official foreign policy of non-interference in other countries' affairs, and about China's public diplomacy*): Of course everybody knows that China still adheres to the principle of non-interference. President Xi Jinping will insist on it. As for public diplomacy, it is very good and it is new. It begun during the presidency of Hu Jintao so I think President Xi will use it. And one thing that is important for New Zealand and to make New Zealand more lovable is, I think, that the New Zealand Government should ask the Chinese Government to give it a pair of pandas. The panda is the best public diplomacy player for China right now.

Professor Zhai Kun answering a question from the audience

What one thing would affect New Zealand's relations with China most?

Cameron Bagrie (*in answer to a question about what one single development might most seriously 'break the connectivity' between China and New Zealand*): What scares the bejesus out of me? We've had three food safety scares in about three to four years, I wouldn't want to go and have a fourth. End of story.

Summing Up

John McKinnon

What a task I have been given, which is to sum up some of today's discussion. I won't even try to do that. Somebody once said the worst possible place to be in a conference is between the conference and lunch. I'm between the conference and going to hear the Prime Minister speak on foreign policy,[1] and I suspect that is an even more dangerous position to be in. In any case, in order to make sure that people can make that appointment, those who are going, I will be brief.

But firstly like Minister Tim Groser may I acknowledge my alma mater, because Victoria University was also a place where I was educated by many of the people in this room and also took my first fumbling steps to learn Chinese with Theresa Wong. A year or so after that I found myself in Beijing. I was in fact in Beijing at the time of the original, well anyway the famous Third Plenum of December 1978, which saw Deng Xiaoping come back to power and many other things happen. And of course like all diligent young diplomats, I wrote a report on that; and unlike what David Shambaugh said I am sure I appreciated the full significance of the Third Plenum at the time that I wrote that report. But as those of you who are from New Zealand or Australia will know, if you send a report to your head office in January it's unlikely anyone will read it, so I doubt whether anybody read my peerless words on the 1978 Third Plenum. However I'm sure they are still there in the files to be recovered by somebody.

David also mentioned that that time was also of course the moment when the US and China established diplomatic relations. I was in Qingdao when I heard that announcement. But a few weeks later I was involved in another event, which was walking down Chang'an Avenue with the supporters of the Democracy Wall movement, a movement which is now almost forgotten but which was closed down by Deng Xiaoping shortly afterwards. And I mention that not so you can make complicated calculations about how old I am but because of that triple effect, the political, the economic and the international all in a sense bound together.

And when we look at the 2013 Third Plenum I think we need to bear that in mind, because the interrelationship between these different facets of what goes on in China is a very important part of the way we have to look at it. Rob Ayson mentioned that we have many different lenses to look at China through, and I think one of the important things about this conference is that it gives you a chance to

---

1   Prime Minister John Key was scheduled to speak at 5.40 pm on 2 July, straight after – though coincidentally after – the 'China at the Crossroads' conference.

both look through these different lenses but also to try and bring them together into some form of integrated whole. That's always difficult because we always tend to bias ourselves towards the particular background and the particular experience we've had.

For that reason I would particularly like to thank our keynote speaker, because David you gave a very stimulating, not to say provocative account of what the Third Plenum is about, what modern China is about, and I'm sure not everybody in this room would agree with everything that you said. That of course is not the point. The point is to stimulate discussion, to stimulate analysis, to stimulate thinking and I think you did that very well. And if I can use what Minister Groser said in another context when he was talking about the concern about the over-dependency on China, it's a serious issue – it deserves a serious answer. The issues you raised are serious issues – they deserve serious consideration. They deserve serious thought. If you disagree with them you need to be thinking very carefully through what the basis of your disagreement is. But in that respect of course we have been immensely helped by the other speakers we've heard from in the course of the day.

And in this respect I think I really would like to acknowledge the role the New Zealand Contemporary China Research Centre has played. Admittedly I was involved at a very early stage in its genesis and don't want to claim too much here. But the Centre was deliberately set up in recognition of the fact that the importance of China for New Zealand requires us to have objective, scholarly, analytical work being done on China in New Zealand, and also to bring overseas experts to New Zealand who can inform us. And that is exactly what has been happening today. I don't know if the New Zealanders in the audience realise just what a wonderful array of speakers we have had here today from the United States, from Australia, from China itself. Admittedly they've been packed into one day and some people may have been rather short-changed, needing more time for their presentations than they were allotted. But you have had a really good slice of what the contemporary academic and scholarly world is thinking about China from many, many different dimensions and I think the Centre is to be commended for actually doing and achieving that.

Now I'm not going to run through all the presentations and give you a summary of them, but I want to make one or two points, just quickly, on each of the panels. The first panel on governance issues I thought was fascinating because it gave you some very fine grained work on some critical issues. Kerry Brown on moral philosophy, Jonathan Unger on rural land, Anita Chan on the trade unions, Stephen Noakes on civil society. All of those told me things I didn't know, and the panelists gave their presentations in a detail which enables you to go away and think about those issues rather more. And that is exactly what should be happening. The fact that some people are producing books on these topics which you can go out and buy is an added bonus to all of that.

Mr John McKinnon from the Asia New Zealand Foundation summing up the day

The second panel was on economic and financial issues, which I think are particularly important for this audience because as a number of speakers just alluded to, these tend to be the lens through which New Zealand looks at the China relationship. And what I think we had there was some really quite fine-grained analysis of the nature of China's economic growth, and what might happen to it in the future, which may not be quite as buoyant as what has happened in the past. This included the rigorous analysis we had from Professor Cai Fang of what the drivers of that growth have been demographically, and what would happen with the *hukou* system if it ever could actually be reformed in a way that might release further productive capacity in the Chinese economy.

I was fascinated by Christine Wong's stories about local government debt, having visited many local governments in China. But I was also interested that when we came to Dr Li-gang Liu in the final session, he provided what I think there is always hope for in conferences like this – a response by saying well, there is a lot of debt, but one way you can deal with this is start a bond market. Now there are lots of problems with local government bonds I'm sure, but at least there you are starting to see how if you probe into these issues, you can find answers to them which are more than just mantras about this and that, about how you've got to reform and so on. So Christine Wong your presentation was very interesting. Professor Ligang Song you were the one who I think got the most short-changed, with the biggest agenda

Summing Up

to cover and probably the shortest period of time to do so in. So I think you are certainly a person I will go back to learn more from.

The final session that we have just had is probably too fresh in everybody's minds for me to attempt to summarise but if I can just pull out of it the fact that here we have a number of people trying to look at what this all means for this country, this 4.5 million people facing a consumer market of 1.4 billion people. And I thought it was interesting what Cameron Bagrie said about the New Zealand economy. You can almost replicate that with China, in the sense that you can take the New Zealand economy, you can look at it through one lens and it looks very positive, you can pick out some other things which are a bit more problematic and when we look at any economy and any polity we are going to have that duality of lenses, and it is how we figure that out that becomes important. That said, I was a little surprised that we ended up talking about love and pandas – thanks Zhai Kun. And thanks also to Marc Lanteigne for keeping us focused on important security issues.

This is probably not the way that a sober academic conference is supposed to finish, but I think there is one other point there that I could tease out. That is that a lot of this is about relationships and how you conduct relationships between one country and another, just as between one individual and another. I think what is really important and what I would like to think has been a characteristic of the way that New Zealand approaches China is that it has done so with a respect for China even though – and Phil Goff made this point quite powerfully – there are a lot of things we don't agree about with China. We don't always appreciate the way China does things and presumably a little bit vice versa. And holding those things in tension, holding the fact that you want a good relationship while at the same time you have to recognise that you are very different societies is a great challenge, and it's one that we are going to have to continue over the next few years.

So I would like to say that I think this conference has provided all of you with not just a series of excellent presentations but also a lot of stuff to take away and to reflect on. And in that respect could I just go back to a comment that was made by Christine, quoting Wen Jiabao's comment about the Chinese economy being unbalanced, unstable, uncoordinated, unsustainable. And I repeat that because it is important to realise that while obviously there are boundaries around the way things are debated in China, there is an awful lot of debate going on in universities, as was mentioned, and in a whole lot of other places in China. It doesn't operate quite as we would imagine it, it's never going to quite do the same sort of things we are expected to do, but it is there.

There is also a huge amount of material coming out of what we talked about earlier – the public diplomacy, the university linkages, the Confucius Institutes. Again you don't have to buy into the propositions of public diplomacy to appreciate that there is now much more information on China out in the world which we all need to discover and consider. This is finally ending as a small plea for my own current job at the Asia New Zealand Foundation, because we are about promoting understanding of China as well as the rest of Asia.

So it remains for me to thank those who served today as panel chairs, Ann-Marie Brady, Xiaoming Huang and Robert Ayson, and again conclude in thanking the New Zealand Contemporary China Research Centre and hand over to Peter Harris to conclude the conference.

Peter Harris

The first thing I want to say, which I think is the right thing to say in these circumstances, is that I agree with everything John just said. Thank you very much for putting all that so much more eloquently than I can do. But let me try and spend just a minute or two before we do draw the conference to a close, to look back as John has done on what we have been talking about today. After all, we convened this conference because we wanted to answer the question, what does the 2013 Third Plenum mean, for China, for New Zealand, for the region and for the world? And I'm not sure that we've really been able to take away an answer to that, though as John said we have at least raised some important questions.

David Shambaugh put forward a brilliant summary from a more sceptical point of view than many would take of what the Third Plenum consisted of, and didn't consist of, more especially of what it didn't consist of. I think David that you used words like opaque or vague or something of that kind to describe the Plenum Decision. I thought that as a helpful counterpoint to that Li-Gang Liu did succeed in outlining some of the specific policies that the Plenum is actually putting into effect. But I think both Professor Shambaugh and Dr Liu, as well as all the other conference participants, would agree that the Third Plenum has not provided a kind of full and detailed blueprint for large-scale reform of the kind that some people hoped. A World Bank report published some time before the Third Plenum that was co-sponsored by the Development Research Centre of the Chinese State Council[2] did go some way towards providing that kind of blueprint and seemed to have the imprimatur of people like the then Premier Wen Jiabao, but we didn't see reference to that in the Plenum.

The other thing that I think we did hear this afternoon in follow-up discussions was a list of the very serious and difficult problems that China faces, problems that no one would wish China ill in trying to address successfully. We heard from Professor Christine Wong how, for example, there are very significant issues of local government debt, which might, as we were reminded, be somewhat resolved by local

2   World Bank and Development Research Centre of the State Council, *China in 2030: Building a Modern, Harmonious and Creative Society* (Washington: IBRD and DRC, 2013).

government bond issues which the Plenum has given the green light to but may not be so readily managed in practice.

We heard from Professor Ligang Song about how natural resource pricing needs to be significantly adjusted, partly so as to deal with the serious environmental problems that China faces. We heard from Professor Cai Fang about how *hukou* or household registration reform is an essential next step to ensuring effective and relatively rapid growth. We heard from Professor Jonathan Unger about safeguards or rather the lack of safeguards still against the state seizure of rural land. We heard from Professor Zhai Kun about the uncertainties and even the confusion – that was a word Professor Zhai used yesterday – about the dialectics – another word he used – of China's foreign policy, seen to be both emollient and also proactive or even aggressive. And last but not least, we heard from Professor Kerry Brown and Professor Shambaugh about the crisis in the Party, a crisis caused by corruption and by an ethical vacuum that is not going to be easy to resolve.

What all this means for New Zealand is I think summed up best in Cameron Bagrie's phrase – was it 'rock and roll' or 'swings and roundabouts'? Either way it is clear that there are going to be unpredictabilities and uncertainties in Chinese policy, not only internally but externally, that New Zealand with all its interests will have to focus on very carefully in the next three to five years. So that in a nutshell is repeating a lot of what John McKinnon so eloquently put earlier, and I think what we have drawn from this conference.

Mr Peter Harris drawing the conference to a close

So again, my thanks to all the great speakers who came from different places and managed to fit into a very small space of time some very stimulating and interesting presentations. My thanks too to all of you in the audience for finding the time and making the effort to come here and listen and take part.

Conclusion: The Third Plenum and New Zealand

Jason Young

'For New Zealand, China is a very significant relationship.' These words, spoken by Prime Minister John Key in Beijing this year, are surely true for most New Zealand commentators. From growth in trade, investment, tourism and educational links to people-to-people exchanges and security cooperation in the Asia-Pacific, New Zealand's relations with China have deepened significantly over the last few years. The debate begins, however, when considering just exactly what this relationship means for New Zealand and what long-term impact China will have on our economy, polity and foreign policy.

The presentations in this volume have provided some insight into these thorny questions. They have done this by creating a frame of reference to understand New Zealand-China relations. The underlying principle is that changes in China, the world's largest developing economy and most highly populated country, can have a large impact on bilateral relations and may possibly reshape the region, thereby changing New Zealand's place in the regional economic and political order. The Third Plenum Decision, therefore, has significant implications not only for New Zealand's bilateral relationship with China, but also as an indication of how China's political and economic development will have an impact on the regional order New Zealand is so reliant upon.

New Zealand's political and economic future is now more tied up with the fate of China than at any time in New Zealand's past. In many ways this is true of many countries, especially countries in Asia. But there is added significance for New Zealand due to its high dependence on external markets and the limited size of our domestic market. Moreover, successive New Zealand governments have actively courted Chinese engagement, asserted an independent foreign policy in a changing economic and security environment, and pursued greater economic engagement with China through trade, investment and business cooperation.

New Zealand's trade with China has expanded rapidly since the signing of the 2008 Free Trade Agreement, with the continued growth of the Chinese economy and its liberalisation since joining the WTO, as well as through the trade promotion efforts of NZ Inc. The goal to double two-way trade by 2015 has already been achieved this year (2014), and a new goal of reaching NZ$30 billion by 2020 was agreed on by President Xi Jinping and Prime Minister John Key this year. China became New Zealand's largest annual trade partner in 2013, purchasing NZ$9.96 billion of New Zealand products, more than 20 per cent of total merchandise exports. Of those exports NZ$4.59 billion or 46 per cent were exports of dairy products. In 2013 9.5 per cent of all New Zealand merchandise exports were dairy products destined for China.

Such statistics have raised the question of whether New Zealand is becoming too dependent on a developing Chinese economy for its export earnings and whether export diversification is required, both geographically and through the types of products New Zealand businesses sell in China. As Phil Goff argued at our conference, having too many eggs in one basket may create risks if New Zealand becomes too dependent on 'a narrow range of primary sector commodities and one market'.

When speaking to our conference, New Zealand Trade Minister Tim Groser addressed this question head on, arguing that the problem New Zealand once faced as it suffered a crippling trade blow when Britain joined the European Economic Community, New Zealand's most vivid historical experience of over-dependency, was due to New Zealand products being shut out of other markets at that time. Today, New Zealand has secured preferential trade access in Australia, Southeast Asia, Hong Kong and Taiwan, and through the Trans-Pacific Strategic Economic Partnership. It is also negotiating in both the Regional Comprehensive Economic Partnership (ASEAN+6) and the Trans-Pacific Partnership. Groser argues these agreements are 'about risk diversification and giving our companies more choice', a guarantee if you like, against any possible challenge in the China market.

In his speech Groser also discussed New Zealand's high level of indirect trade dependency on China, both through import dependency on products required to produce New Zealand exports and through Australia's heavy dependence on mineral exports to China. While this 'indirect dependency' exists, Groser argued, there are 'large practical limits to what we can do about this', with 124 countries now counting China as their number-one trading partner. Chinese importers and consumers offer the highest price for many New Zealand agricultural products and therefore they are acquiring more than 20 per cent of New Zealand exports. If however Chinese consumers were no longer able to pay or did not want to purchase New Zealand products then there are other markets such as Southeast Asia, Europe or North America that exporters could sell to, albeit at what would probably be a lower price than that of current sales to China.

The debate on over-dependency on trade with China therefore relies on two variables. The first is a question of the long-term sustainability of the China market. This question is given a lot of prominence in the presentations collected in this book, with the economists and social scientists taking somewhat different views on how best to answer it. The economists have generally argued that the Third Plenum signals a step in the right direction, though more needs to be done. Their view has generally been that China's economy will continue to develop with a surge in domestic consumption in the middle class. These are positive signs for sustaining

Conclusion: The Third Plenum and New Zealand

Professors Cai Fang (left) and Zhai Kun listening to a presentation

(from left) Professors Jonathan Unger, Cai Fang, Anita Chan and Christine Wong chatting between sessions

New Zealand's trade relations with China. The social scientists in this volume are less sanguine, pointing to ongoing issues of corruption and entrenched interests and offering a general critique of the viability of a market-oriented economy under one-party rule.

The second variable with respect to trade dependency is what could happen if trade with China was disrupted for some reason. Could New Zealand exporters and importers change to other markets in a timeframe that avoided too much economic hardship? Here, we are surely placed better than in the 1970s, but no doubt such a change would again create challenges of adjustment.

Trade aside, New Zealand's economic relations with China have also witnessed growth in investment and services, particularly education and tourism, driven by the rapid development of the Chinese economy and select policy reforms, such as incremental liberalisation of China's capital markets. For this trend to continue, the reform agenda will need to tackle China's most pressing economic challenges. One such challenge, and a major focus of the Third Plenum Decision, has unsurprisingly been the structural transformation of the economy from investment-driven to consumption-driven growth and the realisation of a decisive role for the market in allocating resources. Such transformative tasks will, however, take decades to implement, so the medium-term implications for such fields as investment and services are very hard to predict with any degree of accuracy.

Taken as a whole, the presentations in this volume suggest that the Third Plenum has gone some way to addressing the long list of challenges China currently faces. Some areas, such as financial and fiscal reform, land reform, family planning reform and *hukou* reform, are arguably on the right track and unless there is a major policy reversal it is not unlikely that these key reforms will be pushed through in the coming years and decades. Other areas, such as SOE reform, judicial reform, reform of civil society and environmental governance and modernisation of the military have been signalled as key reform priorities, but it remains too early to tell what the policy direction will be and how much political capital will need to be spent to have these reforms enacted. Other challenges, however, remain missing from the Third Plenum Decision, as Peter Harris and David Shambaugh have both noted.

Overall, it seems to me, the presentations in this book and the Third Plenum documents give a sense of a government in Beijing that is acutely aware of the challenges it faces as it attempts to steer the world's second largest economy and the world's largest single polity through a stage of development that many countries have found themselves bogged down in through corruption and a failure to innovate, thus sinking into the so-called middle-income trap. There is no guarantee this will not happen in China, but the concerted effort to address many of China's challenges that the Third Plenum represents suggests that it is unlikely. Past experience of Chinese reform and the balance of evidence offered in this book suggest China will continue to sustain economic development in the coming decades, particularly

Conclusion: The Third Plenum and New Zealand

in the areas of consumer spending and outward investment, while the speed of its growth will likely slow to a more sustainable and balanced level that should ideally foster a new revolution in innovation and creativity.

As Li-Gang Liu has suggested in his presentation, sustained economic reform and development in China will have a number of major implications for New Zealand. The first is that the rapid growth in China's consumer market will have obvious implications for New Zealand exports to China. Liu believes that in the future 'the New Zealand or Asia-Pacific economy will become more dependent on the Chinese economy', but that New Zealand should not worry about this as its traditional markets should also recover, providing New Zealand exporters with other options. Second, as Liu argues, a product of China's development and the incremental liberalisation of Chinese financial markets will be an increase in the outflow of capital from China. New Zealand has a bilateral swap agreement with the People's Bank of China (the first country to have this) and recently introduced direct trading between the renminbi and the New Zealand dollar. As Liu puts it, 'the renminbi will first be used as a trade invoicing currency, and will eventually be used as a trade financing currency. Once China's capital markets become more open we will see more renminbi-based investment in the Asia-Pacific.' This will have large implications for capital flows, investment and financing for New Zealand companies.

Similarly, Cameron Bagrie has provided us with three messages. First, that New Zealand's structurally impaired balance sheet and demographic pressures mean that it needs to increase its export earnings. With some wisdom and foresight on New Zealand's part, China should be a positive part of achieving that goal. Second, that rising connectivity in the Asian region increases susceptibility and vulnerability, meaning that New Zealand should prepare for peaks and troughs, particularly in commodity markets. Third, while the economic opportunities for New Zealand are taken care of through free trade agreements signed or pending with around 4 billion people, the task today is to have clear strategies for the execution of these opportunities, a trend that Bagrie argues has begun to develop over the last few years.

Overall, then, if managed well the outlook for New Zealand's economic relationship with China in the coming years is broadly positive. But New Zealand's engagement with China and the region is not limited to economics and trade, however positive that story currently is. As Goff has noted, 'Our engagement with China and the balancing of our relationships with China and the other super power in our region, the United States, will more and more become front and centre of New Zealand's foreign and trade policy.' Hence, New Zealand's relationship with China and the region is not and cannot be, to paraphrase former Prime Minister Robert Muldoon, all about trade. We need to remain acutely aware of changing diplomatic and security relations with China in the Asia-Pacific region as China's presence becomes more strongly felt.

China's foreign policy, as Zhai Kun and Marc Lanteigne have both noted in their presentations, has become more proactive in recent years. This creates a challenge for New Zealand, a country heavily reliant on the existing international order, and also presents a puzzle. How should New Zealand interpret China's foreign policy, and also how should it interpret other countries' responses to China's more proactive role? New Zealand scholars are increasingly vocal on both counts. As for our conference presenters, Zhai has suggested a role for New Zealand working with China in regional and international institutions. Lanteigne has been more doubtful, suggesting instead that New Zealand consider tending toward neutralism, a plausible posture for a country whose regional economic and political relations are pulling in various directions.

As Robert Ayson noted during our conference, the many lenses on China's reform trajectory evident in the conference presentations, most strikingly the economic and security lenses, provide very different types of analysis and conclusions. The challenge therefore is to try to bring these strands of analysis together, to understand the interactions between China's political, social and economic reform trajectories and its growing role in the region and to tease out the implications for New Zealand. This is no easy task considering the increasing divergence in views on China, but it is one that New Zealand scholars, policymakers and business analysts must remain attuned to if they are to successfully manage relations with China and others in the region.

As many of our conference speakers would have accepted, trade and security are clearly deeply inter-related. Without a stable regional order it is difficult for economic and trade relations to develop in a stable and steady way. It is therefore in New Zealand's interests for the Asia-Pacific region to maintain and build on the existing regional system that has allowed New Zealand to prosper through regional trade. New Zealand's influence here may be limited on its own but effective if working with like-minded partners. Similarly, New Zealand can play a positive and proactive role in creating new opportunities to cooperate with China, such as through tripartite aid delivery of the kind being implemented in the Cook Islands, and to span what at times appears to be an emerging gulf between economic and security perspectives.

For New Zealand, therefore, the major implications of the Third Plenum Decision are fourfold. First, we are likely to become more dependent on trade with China as the Chinese middle class grows and the structural shift in the Chinese economy toward a more consumption-driven society takes place. New Zealand is very likely to reach the goal of NZ$30 billion worth of two-way trade with China by 2020. Moreover, New Zealand's level of direct economic dependency on China is high but its indirect dependency is even higher. This fundamentally affects any discussion on trade dependency. Any diversification of trade to other countries in the region as a result of unforeseen changes in China is likely to have a limited impact on New Zealand's dependency on China, because these countries will also be heavily impacted by any changes in China, thus reducing though not eliminating options for trade diversification. A high level of trade with China is therefore likely to continue.

Second, we should expect to see an increasing level of Chinese investment abroad, and can and should develop a clearer set of priorities for shaping what type of investment is directed into New Zealand's domestic economy. Whilst it is paramount that New Zealand's regulatory systems continue to give equal treatment to inward foreign investment irrespective of its source, there remains a lot of scope for channelling Chinese investment into areas most useful to New Zealand's economic and social development, and to supporting sustainable economic integration between New Zealand and China.

Third, we should watch closely to see how China's political and economic reforms proceed over the coming decade. While the Third Plenum Decision provided some confidence that Chinese policymakers are addressing many of the key challenges in China's development, there are some challenges that remain problematic and, according to western political theory, fundamental to long-term sustainability. Democratisation is the obvious example here. How these challenges are handled over the coming decades may determine how successfully New Zealand businesses and society are able to interact with the Chinese economy and people.

Fourth, China's growth and development has propelled its economy to a level where Chinese influence in the region and on a global scale will increasingly have an impact on New Zealand's place in the world, even without a high level of direct economic engagement with China. China's economic emergence is reshaping the structure of the regional economic order. With its economic pull China has also become an important diplomatic and security partner in the Asia-Pacific and elsewhere. The dilemma China's leaders now face in addressing the demands these changes entail, discussed by Zhai in his presentation, will continue to be present in New Zealand's relations with China and other countries in the region for the foreseeable future. New Zealand has a number of partners in the Asia-Pacific and will continue to work with them toward the establishment of a rules-based regional order to safeguard New Zealand's legitimate rights and interests in the region. China can become one such partner, as Zhai suggests, though clearly such a partnership cannot be at the expense of existing relations, and vice versa.

To sum up, the likely medium-term impact of the Third Plenum Decision on New Zealand is the deepening of New Zealand-China economic relations, coupled with a continued and perhaps growing need to manage the differences in the two countries' political systems. There will also be a need for New Zealand to manage – and balance – increasingly complex and at times tense relations with China and with other traditional partners in the Asia-Pacific.

A Note on Further Reading

A good historical introduction to contemporary China is Odd Arne Westad's *Restless Empire: China and the World since 1750* (New York: Basic Books, 2012). *Wealth and Power: China's Long March to the Twenty-First Century* by Orville Schell and John Delury (New York: Random House, 2013) emphasises the hard realism behind China's modernising ambitions.

Two useful guides to China and the Chinese Communist system are Anthony Saich's *Governance and Politics of China* (London and New York: Palgrave MacMillan, 2004) and John Bryan Starr's *Understanding China: A Guide to China's Economy, History and Political Culture* (New York: Hill and Wang, 2010). Of the various overviews of the Chinese economy, Justin Lin Yifu's *Demystifying the Chinese Economy* (Cambridge: Cambridge University Press, 2011) comes from a leading Chinese economist who was also chief economist at the World Bank.

On the 2013 Third Plenum itself, the standard text is *Documents of the Third Plenary Session of the 18th Central Committee of the Communist Party of China* (Beijing: Foreign Languages Press, 2013). This booklet contains the Communiqué and Decision of the Plenum as well as President Xi Jinping's subsequent Explanatory Note. These documents are also available online. The Decision in English is at http://www.china.org.cn/china/third_plenary_session/2014-01/16/content_31212602.htm, and in Chinese at http://news.xinhuanet.com/politics/2013-11/15/c_118164235.htm.

Some of the views underlying David Shambaugh's conference keynote speech can be found in his *China Goes Global: the Partial Power* (Oxford and New York: Oxford University Press, 2014). For background to Kerry Brown's conference presentation see his *The New Emperors: Power and the Princelings in China* (London and New York: I. B. Tauris, 2014). For more on the Communist Party of China see Richard MacGregor's *The Party: The Secret World of China's Communist Rulers* (London and New York: Penguin Books, 2010). On the conduct of one former Party leader see Jamil Anderlini's eye-opening *The Bo Xilai Scandal: Power, Death, and Politics in China* (London and New York: Penguin Books, 2012). Anderlini, a New Zealander and a Victoria University of Wellington alumnus, is the *Financial Times* Bureau Chief in Beijing and well worth reading on a regular basis.

On other specific issues, Anne-Marie Brady's *Making the Foreign Serve China: Managing Foreigners in the People's Republic* (Lanham: Rowman and Littlefield, 2003) still offers a unique perspective. Anita Chan, Richard Madsen and Jonathan Unger's *Chen Village: Revolution to Globalization* (Oakland: University of California Press, 2009 (third edition)) is a classic study of changing rural conditions, now updated.

A Note on Further Reading

The essays in *China: a New Model for Growth and Development*, edited by Ross Garnaut, Cai Fang and Ligang Song (Canberra: ANU E Press, 2013), offer important perspectives on China's current economic reform dilemmas. *China's Hukou System: Markets, Migrants and Institutional Change* by China Research Centre Fellow Jason Young (London and New York: Palgrave MacMillan, 2013) is a thorough study of this particular issue.

On foreign policy and China's role in the Asia-Pacific, *China's Foreign Policy: An Introduction* (Oxford: Routledge, 2013) by China Research Centre Senior Fellow Marc Lanteigne provides a valuable conspectus.

On China and New Zealand, *Forty Years On: New Zealand-China Relations Then, Now and in the Years to Come* (Wellington: Victoria University Press for the New Zealand Contemporary China Research Centre, 2013), edited by Chris Elder, offers many insights. So does the same editor's *New Zealand's China Experience – Its Genesis, Triumphs and Occasional Moments of Less than Complete Success* (Wellington: Victoria University Press, 2012). For future developments see Chris Elder and Robert Ayson, *China's Rise and New Zealand's Interests: a Policy Primer for 2030* (Wellington: Centre for Strategic Studies: New Zealand at Victoria University of Wellington, 2012).

Peter Harris

Biographies in Brief

Guest speakers

The Hon. Tim Groser, Minister of Trade
The Hon. Tim Groser was New Zealand's chief negotiator in the Uruguay Round of GATT (General Agreement on Tariffs and Trade) before serving as New Zealand's ambassador to Indonesia from 1994 to 1997. He then served as New Zealand's ambassador to the WTO (World Trade Organization) and as the chair of agricultural negotiations in the WTO Doha Round. He became Minister of Trade in 2008.

The Hon. Phil Goff, Labour Party Spokesperson on Trade
The Hon. Phil Goff held various ministerial positions during the 1984–1990 and 1999–2008 Labour Governments, including Minister of Defence and Minister of Foreign Affairs and Trade. Between 2008 and 2011 he also served as Leader of the Labour Party.

Conference presenters and chairs, in order of conference appearance and book entry

Professor David Shambaugh
David Shambaugh is Professor of Political Science and International Affairs and Director of the China Policy Program at George Washington University, Washington DC. Earlier he directed the Asia Program at the Woodrow Wilson International Center for Scholars, and was Reader in Chinese Politics at SOAS (the School of Oriental and African Studies) in the University of London, when he was editor of the *China Quarterly*. His latest book is *China Goes Global: The Partial Power*. Other recent books include *China's Communist Party: Atrophy and Adaptation*; and *Power Shift: China and Asia's New Dynamics*.

Professor Anne-Marie Brady (*chair of Panel 1*)
Anne-Marie Brady is Professor of Political Science at the University of Canterbury, a Global Fellow at the Woodrow Wilson Center in Washington DC and a Senior Fellow at the China Policy Institute at the University of Nottingham. She is editor-in-chief of *The Polar Journal*, and the author of eight books and more than forty scholarly papers on a range of issues, including China's Arctic and Antarctic interests, China's modernised propaganda system, New Zealand-China relations

and competing foreign policy interests in Antarctica. Her next book, due out in 2015, will be entitled *China as a Polar Great Power*.

Professor Kerry Brown
Kerry Brown is Director of the China Studies Centre at the University of Sydney, where he is Professor of Chinese Politics. He is also an Associate Fellow of Chatham House, London, and a Senior Fellow at Nottingham University and the LSE (London School of Economics and Political Science). Earlier he worked for the UK Foreign and Commonwealth Office in London and at the British embassy in Beijing. Professor Brown's main specialities are the politics and society of modern China and its international relations. His most recent books (both published in 2014) are *Carnival China: China in the Era of Hu Jintao and Xi Jinping* and *The New Emperors: Power and the Party in China*. He is also the chief editor of the *Berkshire Dictionary of Chinese Biography*.

Professor Jonathan Unger
Jonathan Unger is Director of the Contemporary China Centre and a Professor in the Political and Social Change Department at ANU (the Australian National University), Canberra. He is a specialist on Chinese society, rural reform, factory life, nationalism and Cultural Revolution history. He has written and edited fourteen books on China as well as many articles and essays. His work *Chen Village* (co-authored with Richard Madsen and Anita Chan), a history of the Chinese revolution in one village, has been through three editions. He is editor (with Anita Chan) of *The China Journal*, Canberra.

Professor Anita Chan
Anita Chan is an authority on labour, labour conditions and labour rights in China and Vietnam. She is also a specialist in Chinese students and Cultural Revolution history. She has authored, co-authored and edited seven books and a hundred or so refereed articles, including the classic *Chen Village* (see Jonathan Unger above). Professor Chan is a Professor at the China Research Centre at the University of Technology, Sydney, and a Visiting Fellow at the ANU, Canberra. She is co-editor (with Jonathan Unger) of *The China Journal*, Canberra.

Dr Stephen Noakes
Stephen Noakes is a Lecturer in Politics and International Relations at the University of Auckland specialising in contemporary China. His research interests include advocacy networks and civil society, as well as aspects of Chinese law. He is a regular commentator and writer on Chinese affairs for popular media and his research has been published in variety of academic journals.

Professor Xiaoming Huang *(chair of Panel 2)*
Xiaoming Huang is Professor of International Relations at Victoria University of Wellington. He teaches East Asian politics, the international relations of East Asia, and China's politics and international relations. He has written and published extensively on East Asia's political economy, the economic development of China, and the international relations of East Asia. His latest publications include *Modern Economic Development in Japan and China: Developmentalism, Capitalism, and the World Economic System* and *China and the International System*. Professor Huang was founding Director of the New Zealand Contemporary China Research Centre until early 2014.

Professor Cai Fang
Cai Fang is a newly appointed Vice-President of CASS (the Chinese Academy of Social Sciences) in Beijing, having been Director of the CASS Institute of Population and Labor Economics. He is a Member of the Standing Committee of the Chinese National People's Congress. Professor Cai has published numerous works on China's economic and social reforms, including *China Miracle: Development Strategy and Economic Reform*, co-authored with Zhou Li and Justin Lin Yifu, former Chief Economist at the World Bank.

Professor Christine Wong
Christine Wong is Director of the Centre for Contemporary Chinese Studies at the University of Melbourne, and was earlier Professor of Chinese Public Finance and Director of Chinese Studies in the School of Interdisciplinary Area Studies at the University of Oxford. She has also been the Henry M. Jackson Professor of International Studies at the University of Washington. Professor Wong has also held senior staff positions in the World Bank and the Asian Development Bank. She has authored and co-authored numerous books and scholarly articles on China's public finance, including several World Bank studies. She is a member of the OECD Advisory Panel on Budgeting and Public Expenditures.

Associate Professor Ligang Song
Ligang Song is Associate Professor and Director of the China Economy Program at the ANU College of Asia and the Pacific. Associate Professor Song has published, lectured and spoken publicly on many aspects of China's economic and financial reforms. He has authored, co-authored and edited a large number of books and articles on the contemporary Chinese economy, including more than a dozen books co-edited with Professor Ross Garnaut. Dr Song's areas of expertise include environment and resource economics, econometrics and statistics, international economics and finance, and economic development and growth.

Biographies in Brief

Professor Robert Ayson *(chair of Panel 3)*
Professor Robert Ayson is Professor of Strategic Studies at Victoria University of Wellington. A frequent commentator and broadcaster as well as the author of numerous books and articles on strategic affairs, he was Director of the Centre for Strategic Studies: New Zealand at Victoria University of Wellington from 2010 until early 2014.

Professor Zhai Kun
Zhai Kun is a senior scholar at CICIR (the China Institutes of Contemporary International Relations), Beijing. He is Director of the Institute of World Political Studies at CICIR, and earlier oversaw CICIR research on Southeast Asian and Oceanian studies. He has written and published widely on Chinese foreign affairs, including China's relations with Southeast Asia, Australia and New Zealand.

Dr Li-Gang Liu
Li-gang Liu is Chief Economist, Greater China, for the Australia and New Zealand Banking Group (ANZ). In 2012 he was named Economist of the Year by *China Business News*, Shanghai. Earlier he worked for the Hong Kong Monetary Authority, the ADB and the World Bank. He has published widely in scholarly journals, and contributes to *FTChinese.com, Caijing* and the *Shanghai Securities Journal*.

Mr Cameron Bagrie
Cameron Bagrie is the Chief Economist, New Zealand, for ANZ. Earlier he worked for the National Bank of New Zealand and the New Zealand Treasury. He is a frequent commentator on New Zealand economic and financial affairs.

Dr Marc Lanteigne
Marc Lanteigne is head of Asia research at the Norwegian Institute of International Affairs, having been a Senior Lecturer in Political Science at Victoria University of Wellington until July 2014. He is also a Senior Research Fellow at the New Zealand Contemporary China Research Centre. He specialises in Chinese politics and foreign policy and regional international relations. He has published extensively in his fields of interest and written three books, including *China's Foreign Policy: An Introduction*.

Mr John McKinnon
John McKinnon is Executive Director of the Asia New Zealand Foundation. Earlier he was successively Director of the National Assessments Bureau, Ambassador to China, Deputy Secretary of Foreign Affairs and Trade and Secretary of Defence. Starting in January 2015 he will serve a second time in Beijing as New Zealand's Ambassador to China.

Mr Peter Harris
Until August 2014 Peter Harris was Acting Director of the New Zealand Contemporary China Research Centre. Earlier he was successively Representative for China of the Ford Foundation in Beijing, founding Director of the Asia 2000 Foundation (now Asia New Zealand Foundation) in Wellington, founding Director of the Victoria University of Wellington (VUW) Asian Studies Institute, and Senior Fellow of the VUW Centre for Strategic Studies: New Zealand.

Author of Conclusion

Dr Jason Young
Jason Young is a Lecturer in Political Science at Victoria University of Wellington and a Fellow and Programme Director of the New Zealand Contemporary China Research Centre. His research focuses on the political economy of Chinese reform and rural development. He is currently conducting a research project on New Zealand investment in rural China with a grant from the Marsden Fund of the Royal Society of New Zealand. He is the author of *China's Hukou System: Markets, Migrants and Institutional Change*.

About the New Zealand Contemporary China Research Centre

The New Zealand Contemporary China Research Centre promotes knowledge and understanding of China today through support for research, including collaborative research, lecturers, seminars, conferences, the publication of books and research papers, visitor exchanges and information sharing.

The Centre helps build capacity and shares knowledge on contemporary China among New Zealand's universities, business community and public sector. It also promotes informed, effective and sustainable relations between New Zealand and China. The Centre regularly plays host to visiting scholars and delegations from leading universities and research centres in China, and promotes visits by New Zealand scholars to counterpart institutions in China.

The Centre's conference on 'China at the Crossroads – What the Third Plenum means for China, New Zealand and the World' was the fifth in its series of annual Wellington Conferences on Contemporary China. Earlier conferences in the series focused on China's development (2009), China and India – the end of development models (2010), China and Japan in modern economic growth (2011), the Chinese model of modern economic development and social transformation (2012), and China's global course – the political economy of China going global (2013).

The New Zealand Contemporary China Research Centre is based at Victoria University of Wellington and in addition to Victoria University of Wellington it has five university members – the University of Auckland, Auckland University of Technology, the University of Canterbury, the University of Otago and the University of Waikato.

Editor's Acknowledgements

Thanks are due to Tony Browne, Jason Young and Lai Ching Tan for the essential roles they played in planning and organising the 'China at the Crossroads' conference in Wellington. Marc Lanteigne, Gao Hongzhi and Li Dongkun offered helpful ideas and support, and Fergus Barrowman and Kyleigh Hodgson at Victoria University Press gave valuable advice and direction in preparing this book for publication. The ready assistance of student volunteers Hamish Brodie, Luke Gilkison, Ethan Jones, Rainy Liu, Theodore McLay, Gao Yang and Nicola Yong was much appreciated, as was Evan Bo Li's discreetly skilled photography.

The New Zealand Contemporary China Research Centre's thanks must also go to the following for their generous support of the 'China at the Crossroads' conference and events associated with it: Air New Zealand, ANZ Bank, the Asia New Zealand Foundation, Beef & Lamb New Zealand, Business NZ, the Ministry of Business, Innovation and Employment, the Ministry of Defence, the Ministry of Education, the Ministry of Foreign Affairs and Trade, the New Zealand China Council, New Zealand Trade and Enterprise, the Reserve Bank of New Zealand, Te Puni Kokiri, The Treasury, and (last but not least) Victoria University of Wellington itself.

APPENDIX

CHINA AT THE CROSSROADS

What the Third Plenum means for China, New Zealand and the World

2 July 2014

Conference programme

8.30 – 9.00	Registration, coffee
9.00 – 9.10	Introductory remarks by **Mr Tony Browne**, Executive Chair, New Zealand Contemporary China Research Centre, and **Professor Neil Quigley**, Deputy Vice Chancellor (Research), Victoria University of Wellington
9.10 – 9.30	Opening speech by **The Hon. Tim Groser**, MP, Minister of Trade
9.30 – 10.10	Keynote speech: 'China at the crossroads: the Third Plenum and China's reform challenges'
	Professor David Shambaugh, Professor of Political Science and International Affairs and founding Director of the China Policy Program at the Elliott School of International Affairs, George Washington University, Washington DC
10.10 – 10.30	Coffee break
10.30 – 12.15	Panel 1, on governance and society, chaired by **Professor Anne-Marie Brady**, School of Social and Political Sciences, University of Canterbury
	Professor Kerry Brown, Professor of Chinese Politics and Director of the China Studies Centre at the University of Sydney; Associate Fellow at Chatham House London. 'The moral basis of Party rule under Xi Jinping, and the Party's search for a system of ethics in the 21st century'.
	Professor Jonathan Unger, Director of the Contemporary China Centre at the ANU (Australian National University) and co-editor of *The China Journal*. 'The Third Plenum and rural property rights: significant decisions in the right direction'.
	Professor Anita Chan, Professor in the China Research Centre at the University of Technology, Sydney, and co-editor of *The China Journal*; Visiting Fellow at the Contemporary China Centre, ANU. 'The Chinese Trade Union Federation at the Crossroads – relaxing control over labour or risking labour instability'.

	Dr Stephen Noakes, Lecturer in Politics and International Relations at the University of Auckland. 'Civil society and social welfare after the Third Plenum'.
12.15 – 1.00	Lunch break
1.00 – 1.15	Speech by **The Hon. Phil Goff**, MP, Labour Party Spokesperson on Trade
1.15 – 2.45	Panel 2, on economic and financial affairs, chaired by **Professor Xiaoming Huang**, Professor of International Relations, Victoria University of Wellington
	Professor Cai Fang, Director of the Institute of Population and Labor Economics, CASS (Chinese Academy of Social Sciences). 'Demographic dividend to reform dividend: *hukou* [household registration] reform and its impact on economic growth in China'.
	Professor Christine Wong, Director of the Centre for Contemporary Chinese Studies at the University of Melbourne, earlier Professor and Director of Chinese Studies at the University of Oxford. 'Public financial management in China: fiscal decentralization and the challenge of containing local government debt'.
	Professor Ligang Song, Director of the China Economy Programme at the ANU. 'China's resource demand, the environment and enterprise system reform'.
2.45 – 3.00	Tea break
3.00 – 4.30	Panel 3, on international and regional implications, including for New Zealand, chaired by **Professor Robert Ayson**, Professor of Strategic Studies, Victoria University of Wellington
	Professor Zhai Kun, Director of the Institute of World Political Studies at CICIR (China Institutes of Contemporary International Relations). 'Chinese foreign policy in the light of the Third Plenum, with special reference to New Zealand'.
	Dr Li-gang Liu, Chief Economist, Greater China, ANZ. 'The impact of the Third Plenum and other recent policy initiatives on the Asia-Pacific region'.
	Mr Cameron Bagrie, Chief Economist, New Zealand, ANZ. 'The impact of the Third Plenum and other recent policy initiatives on New Zealand'.
	Dr Marc Lanteigne, Senior Lecturer in International Relations and Director of Research in the New Zealand Contemporary China Research Centre at Victoria University of Wellington. 'Sino-American rivalries after the Plenum: New Zealand and regional responses'.
4.30 – 4.45	Summing up and concluding remarks by **Mr John McKinnon**, Executive Director, Asia New Zealand Foundation, and **Mr Peter Harris**, Acting Director, New Zealand Contemporary China Research Centre

Index

Page numbers in italics refer to photographs.

100 percent pure New Zealand 29–30

agriculture 29
  imports 98
  land rights 57–63
  workforce 81–84
Air Defence Identification Zone (ADIZ) 114, 126
Air Force (of PLA) 9
All-China Federation of Trade Unions (ACFTU) 64–71
Association of Southeast Asian Nations (ASEAN) 19, 117–119
Australia 19–20, 25, 28, 127, 128–129, 146
Ayson, Robert *110*

Bagrie, Cameron *110*, *123*
beef trade 24, 28
Bo Xilai 27
Brady, Anne-Marie *52*, *69*, *132*
Brown, Kerry *48*, *69*, *132*
Browne, Tony 10
Bush, George W. 107

Cai Fang *80*, *147*
Chan, Anita *48*, *69*, *132*
Chen Deming 27, 29
China Banking Regulatory Commission (CBRC) 88–89
Chinese People's Political Consultative Conference (CPPCC) 10
civil society 43, 72–76
Clinton, Hillary 107
coal use 29, 98, 100–102
Communist Party
  attitudes to reform 47

Central Committee 7, 55
  control of trade unions 64–71
  corruption in 41, 51
  role and rationale 10–11, 52–56
Confucian thinking 56, 112
consumption growth 113, 115–117, 148, 149, 150
Cook Islands 76, 109, 129, 150
corruption 9, 32, 41–42, 56, 113–114
Council of State Security (National Security Council) 8, 11, 114, 125
crayfish/crustacean trade 24, 28
Cuba 76
currency reform 9, 30, 117, 119, 149

dairy trade 27, 29–30, 121, 122, 146
Daoist idea about New Zealand 112
demographics 29, 79–83
Deng Xiaoping 7, 31, 37–39, 58, 66, 73, 131, 138

education 42, 73, 74, 84, 93, 116, 135–136
energy use 43, 96–103
environment 32, 43, 46, 100–103
ethics and morality 55–56, 109
ethnic minorities 12, 40

Fiji 129
financial system 8–9, 30–32, 46, 114–115, 149
  centre-local fiscal relations 87–95
Five-Year Plans, Twelfth and Thirteenth 83
Fonterra 29–30, 121–123
food safety 29–30, 137
foreign investment (in China) 46, 113

foreign policy (Chinese) 11, 12, 43–45, 107–112, 125–130, 134, 137
  New Zealand's place in 107, 109, 112
foreign policy (New Zealand) 33, 128–129, 141, 149–151
foreign-funded businesses 117
  labour relations in 67, 70–71
forestry exports/log trade 27, 121
Free Trade Agreement, New Zealand-China 18, 21–22, 27, 29, 112, 129

Germany 108
Gini co-efficient 39–40, 85
Goff, Phil *31*
Groser, Tim *20*
growth rates (economic) 23, 30, 38–39, 81–86, 99

Harris, Peter *38, 143*
health care 9, 74, 116
Henan 94
Hong Kong 19, 22, 70
Hu Jintao 41–42, 53–56, 108, 137
Huang Xiaoming *80*
hukou system 9, 32, 39, 79–86

International Energy Agency 103
International Labour Organization (ILO) 65, 67
investment abroad (by China) 117–119, 149, 151
iron ore trade 24–25, 98

Japan 97–98, 109, 119, 125–128
Jiang Zemin 41–42, 51
judicial system 9, 113–114

Kaldor, Nicholas 85
Key, John 17, 145
Korea (South) 97–98, 119, 128
Krugman, Paul 83
Kuznets curve 101

labour camp system 8, 46
labour relations 10, 64–71
labour supply 39, 81–85

lamb trade *see* sheepmeat
land expropriation 10, 60–63
Lanteigne, Marc *110, 127*
Leading Group for Comprehensively Deepening Reform 8, 46, 114
Lewis, Arthur 81
Li Jianguo 68
Li Keqiang 7, 42, 57, 83, 108, 111
Li Zhaoxing 27
Liu Li-Gang *110, 115*
Liu Xiaobo 54
Liu Yunshan 54
local governments
  finances 9, 62–63, 87–95, 114–115, 140
  and hukou system 86
  and judicial system 113–114
  land expropriation 60–63
log trade/forestry exports 27, 121

Mao Zedong 31, 57, 68
Mao and Maoism 53, 55
Maori/iwi businesses 24, 28
markets, role of (in China) 12, 46, 96, 100, 103, 113
Marxism-Leninism 39, 55
McKinnon, Don 23
McKinnon, John *140*
Meng Xin 85
Merkel, Angela 108
Mexico 17
middle-income trap 38, 148
migrant workers 32, 42, 60, 67, 70–71, 81–86
military forces 9, 41
  see also People's Liberation Army (PLA)
Ministry of Finance (China) 87–88, 92–94
Ministry of Foreign Affairs and Trade (MFAT) 30
Ministry of Primary Industries (MPI) 23, 30

National Audit Office, Chinese 88
National Development and Reform Commission (NDRC) 92, 94–95
National Security Council *see* Council of State Security

natural resources 9, 96–103
Navy (of PLA) 9, 130
New Zealand China Council 23
New Zealand economy 98, 120–124
New Zealand Trade and Enterprise (NZTE) 23
Noakes, Stephen *48*
non-governmental organisations (NGOs) 42, 43, 70, 72–76

Obama, Barack 107
one-child policy 8, 32, 46, 114

Pareto, Vilfredo 85
People's Liberation Army (PLA) 9, 44, 126
Philippines 22, 109, 125, 127
political reform 32, 42, 47
political system 10–11, 32, 42–43, 46, 73–74, 133
population policy *see* one-child policy
private sector 10, 32, 70, 113
 rural 57–58
property rights 46
 see also rural land rights

Quigley, Neil *11*

regional disparities 94, 97
rural land rights 57–63, 115
Russia 108

Sanlu 29
Shambaugh, David *40, 45, 132*
sheepmeat 24, 28
Smith, Adam 55
social inequalities 39–40
social security 9, 67, 70, 72–74, 76, 84–85, 116
social unrest 40–41, 62, 64, 69
soft power 43–44, 134
Song Ligang *101*
South Pacific 109, 126, 129
state-owned enterprises (SOEs) 8, 10, 39, 46, 91, 102–103, 113–114, 136
 labour relations in 66–67, 69–70

State Planning Commission (China) *see* National Development and Reform Commission
students (Chinese in New Zealand) 28

Taiwan 19, 22, 43, 97, 119, 128, 129, 133–134
Tang Jiaxuan 27
taxation 9, 32, 74, 75
terrorism 40
Theory of Moral Sentiments, The see Smith, Adam
Third Plenum of 1978: 7, 37, 131
Third Plenum of 1993: 8
Third Plenum of 2013: 7–13, 45–47, 113–115, 131, 142, 146–148
 Communiqué 45
 Decision 8–11, 45–46, 52–56, 57–63, 64–71, 72–76, 114–115
 Explanatory Notes 8, 11–12, 87
Tiananmen crisis 8, 27
Tibet 12, 40, 53
tourism 28, 123
trade, Chinese 97–98, 117–119, 126
trade, New Zealand-China 17–33, 145–146
 New Zealand dependency 18–21, 23–26, 28, 30, 33, 117, 122, 145–148, 150–151
 see also Free Trade Agreement
trade unions *see* labour relations
Trans-Pacific Partnership (TPP) 18–19, 26, 112, 128, 146
Trans-Pacific Strategic Economic Partnership 146

Unger, Jonathan *48, 60, 69, 147*
United Kingdom 26, 28
United States-China relationships 44–45, 76, 107–111, 125–130
universities 135–136
urbanisation 9, 42–43, 63, 83–86, 116
 financing of 92–93
Uruguay Round 24

Vietnam 109, 125, 128

wages 30, 67, 70, 81, 85, 116, 117
Walmart 65, 70
Wang Qishan 41
Wang Yang 69
Wang Yi 111
Wen Jiabao 12, 17, 29, 38, 55, 87, 116, 142
women's issues 135
Wong, Christine 88, *147*
World Bank 87, 101, 142
World Trade Organization (WTO) 21–22
World Wildlife Fund 73

Xi Jinping 7–9, 11–13, 31, 41–42, 68, 87, 107–112, 125, 137
  beliefs 51–53, 56
Xinjiang 12, 40, 53
Xu Caihou 41

Yu Jie 51–53, 56

Zeng Jinghong 51
Zhai Kun *110*, *137*, *147*
Zhou Yongkang 41